Editorial

Your great days are gone, great days are always gone...

Richard Howard cut his teeth as a translator by Englishing two volumes of Charles de Gaulle's war memoirs, *Unity* and *Salvation*, published in 1959 and 1960. The complete war memoirs (1940–46) run to 1,056 pages, and Howard rendered the lion's share. It seems quite a leap from this commission to the several dozens of translation projects that followed, of *Les Fleurs du mal* for which he received a National Book Award in 1983; Roland Barthes's *Camera Lucida, Mythologies* and *Mourning Diary*; Maurice Nadeau's *History of Surrealism*; Simone de Beauvoir 688-page *Force of Circumstance* (she was his one major female project); Michel Butor, Albert Camus, E.M. Cioran, Gilles Deleuze, Michel Foucault, André Gide, Jean-Paul Sartre, Stendhal, and much more. His bulldog, in the 1970s, he called Gide. (His stuffed gorilla was Mildred.)

In an interview in 2004 he declared, 'The practice of translation is essentially, insofar as it concerns writing, a matter of erotic submission, and even erotic imposition.' What a varied and demanding congeries of erotic dominators he submitted to, and what sinuous skills and imaginative responses he devised! With Barthes and Cioran, whose work he translated *in extenso*, he describes 'a certain intimacy, or even an uncertain one,' established over time.

By contrast, 'The writer's relation to his editor and to some extent his reader [...] is essentially filial or fraternal.' He was a significant editor, and knew whereof he spoke: he worked for publishers and magazines and helped to shape the careers of Frank Bidart, Charles Simic and J.D. McClatchy. McClatchy celebrated him on his ninety-second birthday:

I know no one who has done more personally to mentor younger poets – making editing suggestions, publishing their best work. In my own case, Richard was my first reader at a time when I urgently needed his candour and high intellectual standards. Unlike others, Richard does not compete with his students, begrudge them their recognitions, or expect them to turn into disciples and epigones.

Richard Howard believed in his readers. The poems often address us directly in the 'you' they deploy; they make no concessions, the dramatic monologues inhabit the periods from which they speak and take for granted the informing reality of their historic and biographical contexts. His narrative strategies make it possible for alert readers to infer what the causes, occasions and sometimes the vocabulary itself are doing. His monologuers don't realise that they are disclosing more than they mean, or even than they know. Howard has internalised the irony that lesser poets would manifest in a trick of form or style, the intrusion of a voice or tone from a jarring register. He said in his 2004 *Paris Review* interview that he understood the poetic necessity 'of the secret that the speaker, who does not know it, must reveal'.

The 'you' the poems address is not assumed to be stable: as his readers, we change in relation to the speaking voices. His last collection, *A Progressive Education* (2014), reviewed in *PNR* by David Ward, was his least characteristic and one of his most ambitious. 'It consists largely of letters to teachers, composed in verse in the first person plural, from a sixth-grade class, decades ago, at Cleveland's Park School (which Howard really attended).' A return to the first years concludes a long, richly digressive journey.

1969 was his *annus mirabilis*. His third collection, *Untitled Subjects*, appeared with its monologues and was awarded a Pulitzer Prize. His critical study, *Alone with America: Essays on the Art of Poetry in the United States since 1950*, also appeared – a work of enormous critical assurance or hubris, depending on your sense of his inclusions and omissions. He was recognised as – potentially – a major figure.

In the wake of his death on 31 March 2022 at the age of ninety-two, the story of his life was re-told. It was, in its early years, chancier than most in material poverty, his being put up for adoption and losing his birth family and the kinds of memory that parents and grandparents inculcate, the accidentals which supply materials for imagining a personal history. In one poem he speaks of himself as 'a borrowed book'. The missing elements became a core of the narrative of a fortunate adoption which has the intricacy of a good short story.

He received the 2017 *Paris Review*'s Lifetime Achievement Award for his contribution to literature. His criticism, poetry and translations stirred and troubled readers and stimulated change in ways of reading. His impact was not limited to the Anglophone world. The *Paris Review* was celebrating their one-time poetry editor (1992–2005) and Chevalier de l'Ordre National du Mérite, just as dementia was beginning to undermine him. He had put in an exemplary innings and left – especially in the volume and quality of his translations – an unrepeatable legacy. He belonged to a category of writers for whom literature is a passion and vocation, only accidentally a career. As facilitator and practitioner, teacher and critic, he enhanced the world of poetry.

He attended Columbia University and then went on a French government grant to study at the Sorbonne. He recounts how he originally acquired French. It was:

> proposed by a relative sharing the backseat of my grandmother's LaSalle sedan on the way to Florida when I was five. The family caravan (three cars, if I remember) was headed for Miami Beach instead of the annual trip to Europe, which by the mid-thirties had become unfeasible for Jews, especially my people, who were fond of vacationing in the Schwarzwald. My 'aunt' (she was in fact a rather remote cousin) decided to beguile the languors of the drive from Cleveland to Miami by teaching me French *en route*. Her method was to provide an eager five-year-old with the alternative terms for everything we saw out the window and indeed for the window itself, so that by the time we drove up to that neo-Hispanic art nouveau pavilion that was to be our residence for some weeks, I had amassed a formidable vocabulary of nouns and even a rudimentary stock of verbs.

When Charles de Gaulle heard the story he asked his translator how long it had taken him to learn French. 'Five days, *mon général*.'

In 1954, back in the United States, he spent four years in Cleveland and New York working as a lexicographer for the World Publishing Company in the old days of lexicography when dictionaries defined meanings rather than described usage. The job, he said, was 'drudgery, to the point of dentistry', but he confessed in 1982, 'I am grateful to lexicography [...] for inculcating, or at least suggesting, habits of precision and concern with the quality of language on a level that is very important for both poetry and translation, an exacting feeling for the physical shape and size and movement of words as well as for their sense.' This almost *material* feel for the specific word, and then words together in movement on the page and on the air, is a strong discipline against any romantic impulse. Accommodating restraints leads to form and away from the self-privileging 'I'. It is crucial to the literary translator who is after more than just the *sense* of the original.

John Hollander, a contemporary at Columbia along with Allen Ginsburg, had directed him to Wallace Stevens. He found his own way to Auden, who became a dominant influence. Howard speaks of his early poems as 'rewriting' Auden, or writing from within a sense of Auden, an extension of the discipline of translation to the articulation of echo. Finding his way to his own poetry took time, his vehicle being a Browningesque use of the dramatic monologue, submitting himself (again, the erotic analogy) to the person, period and voice of someone not himself, making it real and sometimes, obliquely, making himself real through it, sometimes in the subject matter, sometimes in dialogue. His characters are allowed their prejudices. He trusts his readers' judgement and does not interfere or interrupt. He does not show but lets them tell. Ben Jonson said, 'Speak that I may see thee.' This could stand as Howard's *ars poetica*.

It all comes back to translation, to the dynamics that occur between languages when one submits to another, or between periods, voices, situations. The artist's subjection is at the heart of the process. Does the artist have a voice – 'in fact do I even have a register? I have a modulable energy, a verbality that can be persuaded by what I know or have tried to learn, and a certain mimic gift that allows the reader to suppose (often quite fallaciously) that it is a "distinctive" voice that is raised – or lowered.' He never wielded on others the kind of influence Auden did on him. He teaches but would never subdue: his gift to younger writers is to provide endless resources, hints, gifts.

When in a dramatic monologue he himself needs to invent fact, supply narrative, he honours various givens: known facts, period and milieu, relationships which define a speaker's voice. In the poems, 'nothing is made up and nothing cribbed – everything is imagined and everything realized from what I know and have learned'.

Ford Madox Ford, in his indispensable reminiscence of Conrad, said, 'You must not, however humanitarian you may be, over-elaborate the fear felt by the coursed rabbit.' Also, 'It is obviously best if you can contrive to be without any views at all: your business with the world is rendering, not alteration.' Rendering: this is Richard Howard's achievement as a translator and, at his occasional best, as a poet.

News & Notes

Paz · To mark the 108th anniversary of Octavio Paz's birth, the legendary Colegio San Ildefonso in Mexico City (where the great muralists, Diego Rivera and Jose Clemente Orozco in particular, painted some of their most ambitious works) has dedicated a handsome memorial fountain designed by the Mexican artist Vicente Rojo (who died last year). The work celebrates Paz and his wife Marie-José, who died in 2018.

Paz and Rojo admired one another's work, and the sharp, emphatic red (Rojo) sculptural swirl evokes the ground-breaking *Poetry in Movement* anthology which Paz edited with Ali Chumacero, José Emilio Pacheco and Homero Aridjis in 1966, a book that revealed the wealth of Mexican poetry in the previous half century. The ashes of the poet and his wife are preserved within the memorial. On a granite surface the opening words of Paz's most famous poem *Piedra de Sol* (*Sun Stone*) appear:

Un alto surtidor que el viento arquea,
un árbol bien plantado mas danzante,
un caminar de río que se curva,
avanza, retrocede, da un rodeo
y llega siempre.

Vicente Rojo worked with Paz from 1968. It was a period of political definition, when after the student massacre at Tlatelolco Paz renounced his ambassadorship to India and cut himself free of the corrupted and repressive establishment of the time.

Among other memorable collaborations were the *Discos Visuales* where the reader can reconfigure the words by turning visual discs. Paz provided the words, Rojo the movement and the reader's engagement that goes beyond reading static text, becoming part of the creative process. They also collaborated on the handsome unfolding codex-text of *Blanco*, the *Topoemas* and the Marcel Duchamp box of tricks which was at once a serious and entertaining act of play, in and between forms, objects and languages.

San Ildefonso is an ideal place for the celebratory memorial – an historic building with a long history, open to the public, where the poet can be celebrated every day and by new generations. Paz wrote his famous *Nocturno a San Ildefonso* remembering his student days in the heart of the city.

An uncomfortable irony: the poet's and his wife's ashes were deposited in the memorial by the wife of Mexico's controversial populist president, as though Paz was being re-absorbed into the establishment from which he broke free in 1968.

Minhinnick · On April 22 the Hay Festival – marking its thirty-fifth birthday – announced that this year's poetry medal was being awarded to Robert Minhinnick during the festival proceedings between 26 May and 5 June. The medal has been awarded since the 2012 Olympics which inspired them. 'With Athena as muse, silversmith Christopher Hamilton crafts them locally,' the organisers said. 'Robert Minhinnick is the prize-winning author of four volumes of essays, more than a dozen volumes of poetry, and four works of fiction. He has also edited a book on the environment in Wales, has written for television, and provided columns for *The Western Mail* and *Planet*. He is the co-founder of the environmental organisation Sustainable Wales, and was formerly the editor of *Poetry Wales*.'

Wong May · The poet Wong May received a tenth anniversary Windham-Campbell Prize for Poetry this year. The award coincided with the publication by Carcanet of *In the Same Light: 200 Tang Poems for Our Century*, translations of classic poems with a ninety-eight-page Afterword, described by her editor John McAuliffe as 'a classic meditation on the translator's art, and the art of poetry.' He adds, 'Her translations' syntax and use of the page seem to establish the poem as a single moment, suspending resolution or forward momentum, simply hanging images and lines alongside one another, so that their different notes make up one chord. Or as if the poem's cause, what brings its lines about, is there, coming into view (almost), as each line of the poem follows on and responds to it (and its preceding line – another distinguishing aspect of these poems is how easily we hear the poem's speech and voices as *responsive*).' Other recipients of the anniversary prizes included Tsitsi Dangarembga, Zaffar Kunial and Winsome Pinnock.

PW · In 2022 *Publishers Weekly* is celebrating its 150th anniversary. The editor, writing the editorial for the 276-page anniversary issue, with interviews, reports, an 'anatomy' of the magazine in twenty-five-year retrospects and suggestive prospects, speaks of the ways in which the journal has served 'all aspects of the publishing community', changing as it changes. Its original title, *The Publishers' and Stationers' Weekly Trade Circular*, underlines the kinds of change that have occurred, not least to the apostrophe. A trade which equally served writers and readers – writers could buy their ink and paper from the same store in which they bought their newspaper, magazine and the latest Mrs Humphry Ward novel – has become differentiated and specialised; the variety and quantity of product has multiplied out of all proportion. The issue also includes interviews and profiles, foregrounding twenty-five individuals from the last twenty-five years 'whose mark on the industry is indelible', among them figures crucial to poetry publishing, including poet and novelist Jonathan Galassi (a contributor to *PN Review*, most recently in 2020 remembering the biographer James Atlas; a celebrated translator of Eugenio Montale, and at Farrar Straus and Giroux one of the great publishers of poetry in the United States); Barbara Epler of New Directions, who continued in the ambitious and eccentric poetry and prose directions originally mapped by James Laughlin; the agent Andrew Wylie, who was not wary of poets as authors; and Amazon's Jeff Bezos (originally Jeff Bezos's Amazon), 'who has brought more change to the book industry than anyone since Johannes Gutenberg'. The issue concludes with a survey of the development of diversity in American publishing, highlighting trends and the individuals who are bringing them about.

Nil desperandum! · Some changes in British poetry publishing. The future of Eyewear seems to be threatened by the serious illness of its founder Todd Swift. His collection *Last Poems Before Heart Failure* is described on Amazon in apocalyptic terms: 'Christmas 2021, Todd Swift was in ICU, close to death. His heart had failed. Now, in early 2022, he continues to be tested and treated at the Royal Free Hampstead for this serious health challenge, as he comes to terms with heart failure. He also has a very large blood clot on his heart. With a cover design by artist Edwin Smet, here are a selection of new and older poems, published as a fundraiser for Todd.' We hope that his situation is improving: his authors – wishing him well – also wonder what the future of their books might be. *Nil desperandum!* It has been announced that the poet Don Paterson is standing down as Picador poetry editor after a quarter of a century. It is a list he founded and made profitable with some brilliant and some surprising choices. His successor, the Derry-born and Newcastle-based poet Colette Bryce, will be tasked with continuing his work, maintaining the stable of poets he ably assembled and adding to it. And Bloomsbury has launched its first poetry list under the editorial baton of Kayo Chingonyi. *The Bookseller* says, 'In its first year, Bloomsbury Poetry will release the "heartrending reckonings" of Valzhyna Mort, the "lyrical genius" of Polarbear, the jazz-inflected grief sonnets of Anthony Joseph and the "transformative reflections" of Selina Nwulu in print, e-book and audio editions.'

AGNI · The American magazine *AGNI* is turning fifty this year, an anniversary that is being celebrated with events and publications. The editors declare, 'Our mission remains as it has always been, to bring our readers into the living moment, not as tourists but as engaged participants. And – as means and method – to champion writers who engage the world in and around them.' The event programme is carefully mapped. 'Throughout the year, *AGNI* and Brookline Booksmith are celebrating *AGNI*'s fiftieth with a series of six intimate virtual conversations, all on Mondays at 8 PM Eastern. Each will pair one of the journal's editors with a contributor whose work defines, for them, the ever-evolving *AGNI* aesthetic.' (AGNI, 236 Bay State Road, Boston, MA 02215)

Huws Morys · One of Wales's most distinguished poets, if least-known to non-speakers of Welsh, Huws Morys, celebrated his 400th birthday in April. At the beginning of the eighteenth century, he was well known to his compatriots. He lived at Pont-y-meibion in the Ceiriog Valley, a roadside farmhouse between Pandy and Tregeiriog. He lived a long life, up to 1709, and his mortal remains lie at St Silin Church, Llansilin. He had been church warden there. He wrote poetry for over sixty years and over 500 of his poems survive, though not many are easy to find. Huw was a peerless master of *cynghanedd*, a challenging discipline with strict prosodic, vocalic and consonantal rules and patterns peculiar to Welsh literature. He also practiced in a variety of forms, and whatever he wrote is marked by a joy in his language and its enabling constraints. His anniversary was celebrated with a series of events that foregrounded his places, his life, and his poetry.

Bunyah · The Australian poet Les Murray died in 2019. In May his posthumous collection *Continuous Creation* was published by FSG in the United States and by Carcanet in the UK. The cover image shows Les sitting in the living room of his home, a little farmhouse in Bunyah where the poet farmed, wrote and celebrated God. In a memorial blog, the Scottish poet Iain Bamforth recalled visiting the farm in 1990, a one-thousand-kilometre drive across New South Wales: 'when we entered the bird-shriek of the Bulahdelah forest and Wang Wauk valley in north-western NSW [...] we began to appreciate the significance of "Up Home" and the little homestead of Bunyah. It was where Les's father "was disinherited / for a brother's death" (see "The Mystery" in the present volume, and "The Blame" in *On Bunyah*), a family house that Les had bought back in the mid-1970s in an act of family atonement.'

'What initially drew me to his poems,' Bamforth writes, 'was the uncanny fusion of the deeply archaic and the modern (although many would argue that this discovery of the archaic is the very engine of modernity) as celebrated in the titles of some of the great poems he wrote in the 1970s and 80s: "The Buladelah-Taree Holiday Song Cycle", "Machine Portraits with Pendant Spaceman" and "Walking to the Cattle Place".'

One poem concludes:

We bring nothing into this world
except our gradual ability
to create it, out of all that vanishes
and all that will outlast us.

Steve Heighton · *Evan Jones* writes: Steven Heighton, poet, novelist, translator, and more recently singer-songwriter, died in Kingston, Ontario, on 19 April 2022, after a short illness. He was born in Toronto in 1961, and grew up there and in Red Lake, a small town in Northern Ontario. He completed his BA and MA at Queen's University, Kingston, and travelled and worked abroad before returning and settling into a writing life. He began publishing in the 1980s, short stories, poems, and eventually novels. From 1988 to 1994, he edited the influential literary magazine *Quarry*. His second novel, *Afterlands* (2005), was a *New York Times Book Review* Editors' Choice. He published seven collections of poetry, and in 2016 received the Governor-General's Literary Award for Poetry for *The Waking Comes Late*. His *Selected Poems 1983–2020* appeared in 2021. From the outset, Heighton was the progenitor of a new movement in Canadian poetry: formal, intellectual, transnational, yet never fussy or fusty. His literary ancestors extended back through the canon – and into other languages and traditions, most notably Greek, to which he held a familial connection. His more recent, now final work suggests a building on and development of his early moral energies into broader, more social and political thinking. His 2020 memoir, *Reaching Mithymna*, details his decision to travel to the Greek island of Lesvos to help with the Syrian refugee crisis – and all the chaos of that situation. Not one to be pigeonholed, he released an album, *The Devil's Share*, in April 2021, recorded at Post Office Studio, Wolfe Island, Canada and released by Wolfe Island Records. It is available to stream and download via Bandcamp.

The New Order · *The New York Times* reported on 13 April an event at St Mark's Church-in-the-Bowery so seemingly out of keeping with the poetic traditions and legends of the place that it seems worth noting. This is the church in which the 1997 recital of Jack Kerouac's *On the Road* and Allen Ginsberg's 1994 live recording of *Wichita Vortex Sutra* occurred. The poets were back, but their world and the world itself have changed. The numerous photographs of the dresses worn, the sheer glitter and display, revealed the new order. The *Times* report appears innocent of its own irony. 'Phantoms from a vanishing downtown were summoned to St Mark's Church in-the-Bowery last Friday for the Poetry Project's 55th anniversary gala,' it began. 'The organization is an enduring harborage for New York City poets, and the event brought several generations of the creative community under one steeple to celebrate the spoken word.

'Attendees in suits, gowns, indoor beanies and sleeveless turtlenecks chatted in the side aisles during the cocktail hour. Some wondered if this quasi-formal affair, with $500 seats and a step-and-repeat, squared with the Poetry Project's bohemian past and its association with penniless bards. "There's a little grumbling about, 'How can poets charge money for this kind of thing?'" said Anne Waldman, who was the group's director from 1968 to 1978. "I say we need to keep this place going, and we have to grow up and join the culture." The eclectic list of writers, musicians, actors and designers reflected that outreach. Daniel Lopatin, the experimental electronic music producer who performs as Oneohtrix Point Never, said his favourite poet was Clark Coolidge. "The words are almost nonsense," Mr. Lopatin said. "It's very much rooted in his jazz practice, and I worship him." Next to him was Cory Kennedy, an embodiment of the "indie sleaze" era of the mid-late-aughts, who wore a gauzy tee and pencil skirt, both Calvin Klein. She joked that she was a fan of a contemporary warrior-poet. "Zelensky's not bad," she said. Dinner was served in the nave. A long table near the stage included Chloë Sevigny, Zac Posen, Nate Lowman, Andrew VanWyngarden and Arden Wohl. Leek vinaigrette arrived with mozzarella di bufala and speakers toasted the poetic contributions of Rene Ricard and Patricia Spears Jones. "I think honoring the upsetters"' – by which she seems to have meant the poets who brought the Project into being – '"is important," said Ms. Sevigny, who wore a pink, black and gray ball gown by All-In, which had the confectionary sheen of a raspberry-glazed doughnut. "There's a very cool generation that are now our elders," she said. Dasha Nekrasova, an actress and podcaster, sat a few tables away. She wore a black dress from Brock Collection and darted outside to smoke with a cadre of seatmates. Elsewhere, Paul Slovak, an editor at Penguin Books, sprinkled lore over roast chicken with fava beans. [...] "I think it's a very golden moment for poetry," he said. "There are many, many supremely talented young poets."' It would seem there is also a lot of money in poetry, and that fashion and poetry now walk hand in glove.

'The after-party was held in the back of the church and guests spilled out into a garden patio. Telfar Clemens, the designer, and Juliana Huxtable, the artist, were on hand for theatrical poetry performances and a DJ spinning dance music. Mr Posen, the fashion designer, was asked if poetry might be having a fashion moment. After all, Demna Gvasalia read a poem by Oleksandr Oles at the Balenciaga show in Paris, Loewe cited the poetry of Sylvia Plath as an inspiration for its latest show, and brands like Valentino and Tory Burch recently collaborated with writers. "Clothing can be poetry if worn by the right person," Mr Posen said, "or the wrong one."'

Crufts · *The New York Times* itself had a poetry moment in April, National Poetry Month. The book pages dedicated a whole issue to poetry.

'But first we ask a very basic question: What *is* poetry, anyway?' There is a simple, straightforward answer, not like 'what is a woman'. The *NYT* columnist Elisa Gabbert explained, 'The poem is a vessel [...] poetry is liquid.' The editor chimed in with a canine metaphor, the dog show where 'we might strain to see any similarity between a whippet and a Pekingese and a wire fox terrier, but we recognize them all as dogs'. The variety of dogs in the pages that follow is remarkable. A lot of modish clothing, certainly. As Urban Pup says in its advertisement, 'Dressing your pup for any occasion has never been eas-ier with our on trend, dog clothes. You and your beloved pet pooch can now step out in style with our wide range of in season dog clothes.' For pup and pooch substitute 'poet' at will.

To be fair, there are strong reviews, essays and a few poems, including 'a resonant sonnet about love and war by the Ukrainian poet Yuri Burjak.'

From Angel Hill
Part 1: Translucent Launceston

VAHNI CAPILDEO

Arriving at the top of Angel Hill at dusk in March, you are perched above a street as narrow and steep as one of those 1970s metal slides from which children pitched off, died, and thereafter haunted playgrounds canopied by history-heavy, unpruned trees. To the left you are faced with a stony bank softened by ferns and, even at nightfall, bright with chubby pennywort. To the right, grassier land shelves upwards. Daffodils wave higher than your head, and over the height of shrubby trees. There are also buildings. These seem to have grown according to need and habit. Partway down the hill are three late nineteenth-century cottages in a mini-terrace. They stand together, as planned.

You open the door to the one with a blue plaque on the outer wall, and step down two slabby stone stairs, pausing next to a stand with walking-sticks. If you can open the door, step down, and enter through the next set of doors, you are at a series of thresholds. A sitting-room with knickknacks and a comfortable armchair welcomes you, like someone friendly who was waiting, though not for you. This row of cottages is built into a hill that slopes sideways as well as down, precipitous like a 1950s beauty's shoulder. If you go through to the back, you will continue down slate steps; down and down, past more daffodils, and tulips in raised boxes. But perhaps you are not let in.

As poet in residence, for a month I had the keys to Cyprus Well, the cottage where the poet Charles Causley and his mother Laura lived. Charles died in 2003, but the cottage does not feel as if he left this world. When I return, as I do in dreams, somehow I know that when I return in life, as I shall, someone else will have the keys. I shall walk down the hill, traveller-eyed, knock, and perhaps not be let in. No-one might be at home, except the traces of the two who lived there most; the one who wrote no memoir because his town's life was in his poems; who played the piano, ate and drank and sang. Many people know vaguely of Charles Causley as 'Ted Hughes's friend' or a 'balladeer'. They do not know the man who red-pencilled dynamics onto songs for schoolchildren and left a piano-stool full of Noel Coward and Edith Piaf and the other showstoppers he knew well, as the pianist in a band.

Causley's ghostliness has nothing spectral about it. Anecdotally, most people asked to name their favourite Causley poem choose 'Eden Rock'. In 'Eden Rock' (1988), the adult speaker's parents, impossibly appearing in their mid-twenties on the other side of a stream, encourage him to cross the water to them. In classic children's books of the 1970s – a time that coincides with schoolteacher Causley's late middle age – authors like Pamela Sykes and Nina Beachcroft had presented the threat of being pulled into other dimensions as deathly, a loss of self or substance, entrapment into mist, mirrors, fragmentation. On the contrary, in Causley's own writing, whether for children, or his more complex work, water is wet; his ghosts wear ordinary holiday dress – tweed and ribbons – and invite him to a picnic complete with Thermos flask.

The invitation is to be with your people, steadily in place, despite and – not across, but steeply, almost vertically, through – time. 'I had not thought that it would be like this', the poem concludes. The other side does not wear demonic flummery or celestial finery. Causley's poetics of ghosts are a poetics of home, in multifaceted simplicity, like a clean stream. A photograph of Heaney, Causley, and Hughes, sitting together, intent and relaxed, as only friends and equals can be, hangs in Charles's study. As a reader, I experience the poet Causley as more like Heaney than his friend Hughes.

Whether for Odysseus or the medieval 'Pearl' poet, the beloved dead are on the other side of the river. Having not only read Causley's poem but physically walked his solid stone bridge amidst placid ducks, I would be equally frustrated with readings that reduced his profound precision with locality to the symbolical-mythological or the spiritual-ecological. Towards the end of this piece, I shall offer a different, fourfold reading method. First, however, I shall consider approaches I prefer not to take, but cannot help recalling; and try to recall finding my own way.

In literary non-fiction, and (I am told) in theology, there is talk of 'thin places'. How often these are inaccessible, pristine, or 'lost' places! A thin place: a nostalgia-ridden 'wilderness'. A thin place: somewhere you don't know habitually but feel you know well. A thin place: somewhere sought out in desperation or visited at leisure. A thin place: where we are exempt from knowing anything, from responsibility to anybody, because we can yield to a 'spiritual' dimension, and feel more, other, better, of-this-world-and-not. That is a cynical reading. Yet I reached for the phrase 'thin places' in Charles Causley's town of Launceston.

Sometimes it seemed like a flayed place, not a thin one. Launceston is Cornwall's former capital, the castle reinforcing a river border with grim stone. It is a town where families go into the army or the navy; live in idyllic cottages, in impoverished postcodes. Sometimes it seemed translucent, but not thin. Past and present were – not thick with each other – but quiveringly visible. The atmosphere of Launceston reminded me of the fern girl in the folktale from elsewhere. The fern girl's yellow-green garments showed her thin-skinned limbs through to her pearling bones and the filaments of her nerves and marrow. She was a picture of sensitive depth.

Speaking to people at random, in Launceston's streets,

shops, and churchyards, I found a shared sense of their personal stories being part of the long story of their home. These, of course, are not mine to share. Quietly, they looked both inwards to memory, sometimes to horrors, and out again, taking joy. At St Thomas's church, people check the graves, with the air of calling on their families. I was shown an incredibly ancient carving of the town crier on one side of the church entrance; a carving of a lamb on the other (I patted its stubby tail). It was remembered that news used to be announced from that post. Wild strawberries grew under yew trees. Nobody 'foraged' them. A wild variety of birds sang from all sides.

Perhaps it was waking for a month in the surround sound of birdsong that made me think of applying a fourfold reading technique to Causley's poetry, among others. This technique is adapted from *lectio divina*, a monastic practice. In my non-authoritative adaptation, I read, or listen to the poem being read, out loud. I am paying attention just to a single word, phrase, or image that stands out. I am not looking for an examination-worthy meaning, or a deconstructible pattern. What matters is pace: the reading is slow, the response quick and simple, without justifications or opinions. If what stands out is the word 'and', then 'and' is what I take

and offer. In a group setting, this shakes the poem into a set of initial responses, plain and surprising. In the second reading, we listen for something significant; something that seems to have a deeper meaning. Again, we share observations, without elaborating too much. The third reading involves you in the scene. What would you say to one of the people or creatures in the text? What would you ask, or tell them? Sometimes I want to speak to what hasn't been named but must be there: a bird, a Norman or Quaker ghost... The final reading is least like monastic *lectio divina*; I 'listen' for a point of resonance with my life, or an 'action point' for my creative practice.

A following piece for *PN Review* will look, fourfold, at Charles Causley's poem 'Angel Hill', alongside other writings. If a few people try a fourfold reading together, and are willing to play honestly, what emerges is different from the 'close reading' which stares at a text in the void. I keep outlining, or delving into, approaches to 'slow reading', because it is so productively shareable. It is situated amongst readers, including presence as part of the critical process. The poem becomes known as something shared by echoes and gleams. The words are a place to be alive.

An Incomplete Portrait of Jeff Fisher

JULIA BLACKBURN

J.F.: I think your main concern is to make me seem like an articulate and scary person. Good luck.

When I had completed *The Woman Who Always Loved Picasso* (Carcanet, 2019) I showed the poems to my friend and almost neighbour Liz Calder. Liz said they would work well with drawings and why not ask Jeff Fisher who had recently come to live close by. She has known Jeff for ages: he did a lot of the covers for her when she was running Bloomsbury, starting with the anthology *Soho Square One*, which appeared annually, always with a complex new image and Jeff's variation on Bloomsbury's logo of a female goddess with bow and arrow. Explaining the nature of their working relationship, he says '*she let me be completely in charge of how a cover could be and maintained religiously that everything I produced was the best cover in the history of all covers.* For the Bloomsbury Classic series which eventually ran to one hundred titles, Liz would simply send him the book and he'd reply with an abstracted and beautiful design, *I have a fascination for pattern and would happily keep inventing them until time stood still.*

Jeff has also been responsible for all the posters during the seventeen years of the *Flip Literary Festival*, which is held in the town of Paraty on the coast of Brazil, as well as for the four years of its English version, *Flipside*. This is not to mention his work for a number of other publishers, including the European ones who often send him carefully worded and completely inscru-

table synopses which he enjoys reading; three illustrated children's books; a circling torrent of words crawling like insects around the outside and the inside of a big china bowl celebrating one of Liz's birthdays, and a label for Brazilian liqueur called cachasa, which is made out of sugar cane by a woman called Maria Izabel who lives by the sea in the bay of Paraty.

Liz said Jeff was very straightforward. If he liked the poems he would do something and if he didn't he would certainly say so. If he agreed to take them on, then I must keep quiet and let him do whatever he wanted, trusting that he'd come up with something wonderful.

I gave the poems to Jeff and he liked them. I went to visit him and his wife Christine in their home which overlooks the glittering expanse of a tidal estuary; the air loud with the cries of wading birds, *essentially we bought a view rather than a house.* We drank tea and he showed me some of the paintings he has been doing since he came here, most of them variations of the view towards the estuary *it's a new direction for me. I'm struggling with how to approach nature. Type/image/language is where I'm going.* The paintings are precise and almost classical in style, but always transformed by a single word marching across the landscape or a gathering of words creating a frame around it. The words seem to give a surreal dimension to the reality of what is being represented and they jolt you into an unexpected line of thought, or way of seeing.

We hardly spoke of the poems and what he might do with them but I lent him the catalogue for last year's *1932* Picasso exhibition at the Tate, which had been the initial trigger for writing them, along with the third volume of John Richardson's magisterial biography which has a photograph of Picasso on the cover, his black eyes staring out at his audience with a theatrical and almost manic intensity.

Nothing happened for two months and then Jeff sent me a PDF of three drawings that were nothing like what I had imagined they might be. I panicked slightly, but kept quiet about my panic. I went to see him again and he seemed a bit glum and said he was not happy with what he had done, he thought he'd been too much in awe of Picasso. We talked briefly about the type of images associated with Victorian alphabets in which A is an Apple and B is a Baby and he brightened up and said he'd give the thing another go.

A few weeks later he sent me a PDf of drawings for all forty-three poems, including the last one which is more a list than a poem. The drawings were all numbered and had been given the curiously off-piste but

utterly appropriate titles he had chosen for them, written in his own very particular script. I was in the limbo of an airport lounge when I opened the PDF and tears came to my eyes because the drawings were just what I had hoped they might be, even though I had no preconception of what I was hoping for.

Later I queried the figure of Madam Death who seemed a bit demonic and earth-bound and Jeff quickly changed her so that she floated horizontally towards Picasso, apparently buoyed up by the translucent bubble of her dress. We both thought the drawing of a woman sitting in front of a stack of paintings would make a good cover, but Christine pointed out that, as they were, the paintings could just as well be a pile of sticks and so he tilted them slightly to reveal a bit of the painted surface of the canvases. When he had finished the cover, he wrote to say he was pleased with how it had come out, especially the vivid orange of the background. Job done.

When I asked him, for the sake of this interview, quite what he liked about them, he wrote in an email, *Lately I don't do poetry, I had a younger enthusiasm for it, but these days I equate it with the mystery of cryptic crosswords. Life can be too short.* The Woman Who Always Loved Picasso *appealed to me as a direction I wouldn't normally go in. I didn't have an interest in that period of Picasso's work and couldn't imagine how I could possibly approach it. Julia's snapshots were the opposite of cryptic crosswords and we found a solution. Clearly life is poetic.*

Jeff was born and brought up in Melbourne, as was Christine. He studied film and animation at art school, but didn't like the joint activity that was an essential part of film-making and so he drifted into illustration *for the sake of being solitary.* As a precursor of what was to come, he found he really liked doing handbills for Rockabilly concerts. He says he was influenced by twentieth-century children's books, Arthur Rackham, Ardizzone, etc. *Then I came to London, blah, blah, blah.*

The two of them arrived in London in 1982 and he started his career as an illustrator. Again there was a problem: he didn't want to be involved in what he called the process of graphic design and publishers tended to commission an image to go with a book and then they'd slap their own graphics on top of it. In those days graphics usually meant the joys of Letraset.

The change came when he heard that a new publishing company called Bloomsbury were looking for an illustrator, somebody who would give their imprint its own distinctive visual signature. He met Liz Calder in 1984 and worked on her books until she left the company and moved to Suffolk in 2005. He always used hand lettering for the title and the author as part of the overall design, generally starting with a very rough layer of pencil underneath for the letters, *and then you just plunge into it and it's a matter of luck if it works ok.*

He likes to read the books he is making the cover for, but as he explained recently in an afterword about his iconic cover for *Captain Corelli's Mandolin*, he realised that *one is more likely to engage with an audience the less one confronts them with difficult or awkward choices, things like colour combinations that maybe are not to someone's taste, or depictions of the characters in the book that don't correspond with the reader's vision. It's always much better to not get it wrong than try to get it right. The success of the* Captain Corelli *cover seemed to confirm this. The predominant blue and white spoke of Greek sunshine and the silhouettes muttered romance, war, Greek ceramics, the sea, music and nothing but a vague indication of what the book might contain.* When we were talking, he added that *Corelli is almost monochrome. I think that helps, it is quite simple. There's a relaxed feel to it and that helped too.*

He also said that the first version he did for the book was not bad, *but it didn't have the right feel to it. If I had used that one, perhaps Louis de Bernières's life would have been different.*

And so life goes on. Every day the glistening mud flats on the estuary are revealed and then covered over by the rising tide of the North Sea. The birds arrive and make themselves busy and then many of them set off to the other countries that are also their home. Talking about the mysterious process of coming up with a new idea, Jeff says, *I don't think it ever gets any better, any easier.* I'd happily buy that as an artist's articulate and scary statement on his life's work.

Laughter in the Dark

MARTIN CASELEY

In the poetry and prose of Charles Simic, absurdity and chaos flicker up and flame with sudden recognition. Not just chaos, either: news bulletins chirp away with death statistics, unprincipled decisions, politicians opting for expediency, a public indifferent or filled with hatred... all this might be termed the natural background noise of Simic's surrealism. Except it's not tagged and filed as surrealism any more: our still, emptied cities are de Chirico landscapes and it's just the shrug of 'new normal' background ambience, no longer disturbing or even noteworthy.

Catching up on some of Simic's recent collections – they come thin and fast – one enters a landscape of alienation, desire, park benches and outcasts. Meanwhile those in power rule with their familiar disdain, their barking edicts meriting only a snarled dismissal. In the essay 'Orphan Factory', collected in *The Life of Images* (Ecco Press, 2015) Simic recalls his dying mother enquiring of the wider world: 'Are those idiots still killing each other?' This was in 1994, during the break-up of Yugoslavia, and the poet had already in his youth been a displaced person and an immigrant, but her comment also carries the broader punch of a synecdoche, or the widespread authority of a saw or proverb. Yes, we sigh; the idiots are still killing each other; now, let me hear the headlines.

The humour in Simic prevents this becoming just a depressing experience: there is laughter and recognition in his acceptance of the precise absurdity of this world, a cartoon strip pencilled in by Saul Steinberg. Too much realism dissipates in sketchy backgrounds: comic strip tragedy is an everyday occurrence, the events of history enrolling all hapless spectators as actors, barflies, bystanders as the great events rush by in a mad parade. As he puts it in the poem 'Cameo Appearance',

'I had a small, nonspeaking part
in a bloody epic. I was one of the
bombed and fleeing humanity.'[1]

To Simic, this world is impossible to comprehend in a rational way. As his analogous discussion of Buster Keaton puts it, 'Reality is a complicated machine running in mysterious ways whose working he's trying to understand' (*The Life of Images*, p. 157). Other actors may snarl and shrug, but Simic's sardonic detachment should not be mistaken for fatalism: there is still the attempt at comprehension and, if all else fails, the need to document the fools and fatalities.

Recent collections have seen Simic continuing to employ an elegiac tone when viewing this from his bench. 'Past the Cemetery' in *Scribbled in the Dark* (2017),

for example, acknowledges the 'daily horrors', but finds salvation in the simple sufficiency of a modest meal before that beckoning bedtime. 'Night Owls', another poem in this collection, finds the poet numbering 'fellow sufferers', aware of the machinations of 'a dissembling God'. These moments of awareness are small gains, but closing time in the western world has rarely been so elegantly held at bay.

Like Keaton, Simic is a stoic. He moves, a trespasser within a world of absurdity, without cracking a smile; his family memoirs record atrocity and political demagoguery, and the effects of these. The interiors in his brief, scribbled reports are places where barflies shrug at the relentlessness of it all: 'Nothing new ever happens, / the innocent get slaughtered / while some guy on TV makes excuses...' ('Roadhouse').

As Simic says, 'If you seek true seriousness and you suspect that it is inseparable from laughter, then Buster Keaton ought to be your favourite philosopher' (*The Life of Images*, p. 161), a judgement that Samuel Beckett, who famously worked with Keaton at the end of his life, might endorse. 'Comedy is a serious business' – one of Keaton's phrases[2] – and the same deep sense of melancholy underlies both Keaton's films and Simic's deceptively minimal poems.

Nevertheless, both Simic and Keaton share a sense of helplessness and a certain bemused innocence as they negotiate the surreal landscapes around them. Keaton pursues a determined and logical course in films like *The General* (1926), but he is pitched against a whirling sea of troubles: this also happens in earlier films like *Cops* (1922) and *Our Hospitality* (1923). Apart from the athleticism and technical mastery Keaton demonstrates within every situation, the main joy of watching them is in watching his features: renowned as 'the Great Stone Face', he never cracks a smile. Simic rightly isolates his 'composure' as the truly disturbing, entirely characteristic feature in his protagonists, an almost mystical stillness. Smiles will pass: the train will tumble from the tracks, the idiots will, sooner or later, want to start killing each other again.

Simic's adversaries and companions are pigeons, priests, old hounds, a stuffed parrot, a bartender with a crooked back, a scarecrow, chickens, the devil. Nothing that would faze Keaton, but all of these items are props that could easily be encountered in a frenetic chase scene or populate an interior of comic misunderstanding. The Simic poetic landscape is at once deeply serious and absurdly, comically random: in certain poems, it is also explicitly like a film. In 'The Movie', for example, childhood is 'an old silent movie' as the poet watches a dreamlike film full of mysterious symbols – an arriving

---

1 'Cameo Appearance', *Walking the Black Cat* (1996); all other Simic poems quoted are from *Scribbled in the Dark* (2017).

2 Tom Dardis, *Keaton: The Man Who Wouldn't Lie Down* (Penguin, 1979), p. 131.

ship, a letter being written – all familiar plot indicators. Afterwards, however, we are told this takes place in 'an occupied city' and that the streets are 'treacherous', compared with the briefly lit, magical screen.

In the elegaic poems at the end of *Scribbled in the Dark*, Simic anticipates sleep and darkness – not for nothing is one of the poems in the volume entitled 'All Gone into the Dark'. In this, night owls are 'eyeballing time and eternity', but the same kind of stoicism one sees in Keaton's expression, after enumerating the burglars and the mystics as 'fellow sufferers', can advise only the balm of sleep. Perhaps daylight will disperse the nightmares and will reveal some kind of resolution, or even, as the credits roll, a happy ending.

In the bar, the surreal juxtapositions continue: a group of people eagerly roll a statue towards the harbour; trains dive into rapids; rioting mobs invade the White House. Any minute now, bells clanging, Sennett's Keystone Cops will squeal around the corner.

Four Decades of *The Frogmore Papers*

JEREMY PAGE

Back in the early eighties, when times were tough and jobs were hard to come by, a group of young people recently graduated and with creative, mostly literary, aspirations fell into the habit of convening daily at the Frogmore Tea-Rooms in their hometown Folkestone, once-owned by legendary Channel swimmer Sam Rockett and once frequented by H.G. Wells. There, over coffee and teacakes, a plan was hatched to start a literary magazine with a view to providing a vehicle for the publication of work by their known associates, and in May 1983 the first issue of *The Frogmore Papers*, typed on a manual typewriter, photocopied and black and white, its front cover depicting a group of earnest ancient Greeks, appeared. In September the *Papers* will publish their hundredth number, in their fortieth year, having appeared regularly, for the last several years bi-annually, since that landmark first issue. Time, perhaps, to reflect on the goals the founders boldly – some might say loftily – identified for their fledgling publication: *to publish work which, above all else, possesses quality and a respect for the written word; which uses words to subvert, to innovate, to communicate ideas relevant to the age, articulately, undogmatically, with clarity, integrity and vision.* No pressure then! Thus was a high bar set, and if the *Papers* have not always achieved the standards they aspired to, they have certainly provided a forum for many a new and emerging writer over the last four decades, as well as enabled some more established practitioners to consolidate their reputations a little further and, occasionally, reminded readers of the work of some of the unjustly neglected. In the early years, contributors mostly hailed from Kent and the South East of England, but as the *Papers* became more widely known, writers from further afield began to submit, and work by poets such as Elizabeth Garrett, Geoffrey Holloway, B.C. Leale and Dorothy Nimmo was published. The nineties saw poems by an eclectic group of writers that included Elizabeth Bartlett, Linda France, Matthew Mead, John Mole, Katherine Pierpoint, Peter Russell and Carole Satyamurti, as well as early work by Linda Chase, Jill Dawson, Sophie Hannah, Tobias Hill and Andrew Waterhouse appear in their pages. Attracting the interest of writers of prose had always proved harder, but in the year 2000 Brian Aldiss was persuaded (in the course of a barbecue in Old Headington) to contribute a short story, while the role-call of distinguished Frogmore poets was further swollen by Judith Kazantzis, Alexis Lykiard, Jeremy Over, John Whitworth and Susan Wicks. In the ensuing two decades the *Papers* were proud to feature poetry by Stewart Conn, Sasha Dugdale, Jonathan Edwards, Carrie Etter, Frances Leviston, Maitreyabandhu, John McCullough, Kim Moore, Helen Mort, Clare Pollard, Joe Sheerin and hundreds of others, and pleased to increase the space given to prose and artwork in their pages.

It is some years now since the *Papers* moved their centre of operations from Kent to East Sussex, where a small team assists founding editor Jeremy Page in sifting the many hundreds of submissions of poetry and prose that are received for each issue. To have weathered the storms of nigh on forty years as an independent publication without recourse to grant support does seem like an achievement of some kind, and the hundredth edition will be celebrated with an appropriate launch event in Lewes in the autumn. For some years now the *Papers* have been a truly international publication, with regular contributions from mainland Europe, Australia, Canada, South America, the USA and beyond, and as they enter their fortieth year the aspiration is to continue to provide a platform for any writing of genuine quality, whether 'experimental' or more traditional in form, in verse or prose, from writers known, unknown, or once known but now unjustly neglected, from all corners of the world.

Letter from Wales

SAM ADAMS

Ruth Bidgood, poet and local historian, died in January in her hundredth year. We met a few times, in crowded gatherings, the last, I think, in 2011, when she was awarded the Roland Mathias Prize for *Time Being,* her twelfth collection of poems. I recall the discussion in committee that preceded the occasion and the unanimous choice. Such is the charm of alphabetical order, her poems rub shoulders with mine in several numbers of *Poetry Wales* in the late 1960s and early 1970s, when Meic Stephens was editor. She contributed to four of the five 'ordinary' numbers when I briefly took over the editorial chair and went on contributing to *PW,* the *Anglo-Welsh Review* and *Planet* over the years that followed. You might expect we should have been well acquainted, as I was with many writers who lived across south Wales at that time, but not in this case. Her home was a long way off, along mostly country roads that prohibited ease of contact. Even when, somewhat later, I had responsibilities in what became Powys and travelled quite widely there, I rarely ventured beyond Builth into the remote fastness where she had made her home.

Daughter of a Welsh-speaking Anglican clergyman and a former elementary school teacher from Somerset, she was born in the small, anthracite-mining village of Seven Sisters, near Neath, at the western edge of old Glamorgan, and educated at Port Talbot Secondary (ie Grammar) School. There she was taught by a highly influential English teacher, Philip Burton, whose surname was borrowed by a fellow pupil, Richard Jenkins, when he embarked on his acting career. Ruth Evans, as she then was, went on to read English at Oxford University, graduating in 1943, just in time for call-up. She joined the WRNS, learned how to encrypt and decrypt messages, and served in Alexandria as a coder. Demobbed, she worked, married and settled in and about London. In the early 1960s, with three children and the pattern of her life seemingly established, a small legacy enabled her to realise a long-held ambition – to renew a connection with mid-Wales first formed years before, during her school days. A family holiday home was purchased in Abergwesyn, a hamlet of scattered dwellings around the confluence ('aber') of a stream named Gwesyn with the larger Irfon in an obscure north Breconshire valley. It was a small, inexpensive bungalow, called Tŷhaearn ('Iron House'), for the perfectly sound reason that roof and walls were clad in corrugated sheeting. Whether it was the magnetism of this Welsh home from home drawing her that pulled the couple apart, or some deeper-seated failure in the relationship, the marriage eventually ended in divorce and Ruth came to live permanently in Abergwesyn.

The urge to write accompanied the discovery of Abergwesyn and, in consequence, she belongs to that rather small group of prominent late-flowering poets and authors. She was well into her forties when her earliest poems and prose contributions appeared in journals like *Country Quest* and *Country Life*, tailored to their readership, and the *London Welshman*, which she had known from her London years, but she soon began a productive relationship with literary magazines based in Wales. 'Warning', the first of her poems to appear in *Poetry Wales* (the Winter 1968 number) is unusual in being overtly concerned with personal relations, changed circumstances, new departures. It is also essentially feminist in character:

> Father warn your son against women,
> for are they not the enemy
> whom you were bred to fear,
> the draining mouth of succubus,
> the devil in the thighs?
>
> Teach your son tricks of daily combat
> to defeat these curious creatures...

She was unusual at the time in rejecting classification as a 'woman poet', and refused to be anthologised as such. 'The Given Time', title poem of her first collection, in 1972 from Christopher Davies (then publisher of *PW*), plays with the sense of a new beginning in the context of a scene, an abandoned house slowly returning to nature, that encapsulates a burgeoning interest in the historic and rural:

> That could have been my time –
> The years to come, all meaning gone
> From the broken shape of the house,
> Blurred like a thicker shadow
> Than tree-shadows...
> Not a memory left, not a line of its story.
>
> But in this time decreed as mine,
> With hardly a stone yet fallen, the house is lapped
> By the first waves of forest-land...

With a history extending into medieval times, Abergwesyn was two settlements either side of the river, each with its parish church, both more recently ruined, one now demolished. Depopulation affected rural communities in mid-Wales before and during the nineteenth century and, later, reservoirs filled empty (or emptied) valleys. R.S. Thomas steered clear of the latter (they were 'places in Wales I do not go') and bore witness to the former, ' ... gardens gone under the scum / Of the forests, and the smashed faces / Of the farms with the stone trickle / Of their tears down the hills' side.' But, for Ruth Bidgood, this hamlet in the 'green desert' at the midriff of Wales quite unexpectedly became the source of both fascination and inspiration.

Little of distinction, the guidebooks had said –

A marshy common and a windy hill;
A renovated church, a few old graves
...
And past the church, a house or two, a farm,
Not picturesque, not even very old.
And yet, the day I went there, life that breaks
So many promises, gave me a present
It had not promised – I found this place
Had beauty after all.

Another early poem, 'Roads', which has been taken up and reprinted by others, underlines her sense of separate existence, engrossed in the particularities of the place:

No need to ask where other
          roads might have led,
Since they led elsewhere;
For nowhere but this here and now
Is my true destination.
The river is gentle in the soft evening,
And all the steps of my life have
          brought me home.

A late starter then, but once started, she became a quite prolific writer. On the one side we have the prose products of assiduous environmental observation and research into local family histories – articles, pamphlets and books (notably *Parishes of the Buzzard*, published by Gold Leaf, 2000); and on the other, fifteen mostly substantial collections of poems. All are listed in Matthew Jarvis's important Writers of Wales study (University of Wales Press, 2012).

As might be expected she brought away from Oxford a high regard for Wordsworth and Edward Thomas and, given the deep countryside she made her home, it is not surprising that commentators have seen their influence in her poetry. I hear echoes of Roland Mathias. Nor should that be a surprise, since for both apprehension of place was invariably accompanied by a sense of human history. The dramatic utterance of 'Burial Path' is very like:

When we carried you, Sian, that winter day,
over four rivers and four mountains
to the burial place of your people,
it was not the dark rocks of Cwm-y-Benglog
dragged down my spirit...

There are extensions of poetic reach to other places, people and times, but essentially she concentrated on what she observed and what historical investigation revealed beyond the garden gate of her home. There she found community and dug deep to memorialise its character and its characters. Her poetry, conversational in tone, moves with clarity and composure to add, as Matthew Jarvis remarks, a touch of glory to the ordinary.

Foreground and Background

GABRIEL JOSIPOVICI

Karenin's Discovery

Chapters 8 and 9 of Part II of *Anna Karenina* form a, perhaps *the*, crucial turning-point of the novel. What has until then been tacit, barely acknowledged, now comes out into the open as Karenin decides to confront his wife with the fact that her actions are giving rise to gossip in society; and then, when he actually confronts her, both discover feelings in themselves and in the other they didn't know existed.

The four or five pages this takes are a perfect example of Tolstoy's narrative art and of his ease with the conventions of nineteenth-century fiction, with the unobtrusive narrator guiding us into the depths of the characters' thoughts and emotions within a well-realised setting:

> When he reached home he went into his study, as usual, and seated himself in his armchair, and opened a book on the Papacy at the place marked by a paperknife. He read until one o'clock, just as he usually did, only now and again rubbing his high forehead and jerking his head, as though to drive something away.

Eventually he puts down the book. Anna has still not returned from her dinner-party. He goes into the bedroom, now openly troubled by conflicting emotions:

> He experienced a sensation such as a man might feel who, quietly crossing a bridge over a chasm, suddenly discovers that the bridge is broken and the abyss yawns below... For the first time the probability of his wife's falling in love with anybody occurred to him, and he was horrified.
>
> He did not undress, but paced up and down with his even step over the echoing parquet floor of the dining-room, lit by a single lamp, over the carpet of the dark drawing-room, where a solitary light shone upon the large, recently-painted portrait of himself hanging above the sofa, and on through her sitting-room, where two candles burned, illuminating the portraits of her parents and woman friends and the pretty knick-knacks on her writing-table, so familiar to him. Through her room he reached the door of their bedroom and turned back again (p.158–9 in Rosemary Edmunds' 1954 Penguin translation).

The calm, unhurried pace of the narration, mirroring Karenin's unhurried perambulation through the apartment, effortlessly conveys his thoughts as well as describing for us the *ambiance* in which he and Anna live, but at the same time it manages to convey to us things about Karenin and his wife of which neither of them is aware. As with the listener to a Beethoven piano sonata or symphony, the reader here is given the sense of being able to let himself go and to let the narrative take him along with it, confident that it will lead him deeper into himself as well as into the story. Every detail is significant yet is so intimately a part of a fully realised continuum that it is only at a second or third reading or hearing that we start to see just what the novelist or composer is up to.

What Tolstoy is conveying in these two passages is both the solidity and comfort of Karenin's way of life and the way it has bolstered and reinforced what is probably an innate tendency to selfishness and even to smugness. He settles down in *his* (i.e. his habitual) armchair to read a book that has nothing to do with his life yet is not some frivolous novel but rather a serious work of history. However, something is troubling him of which he is not even aware. As usual he goes on reading till one o'clock in the morning, 'only now and again rubbing his high forehead and jerking his head' – and now Tolstoy ventures something more than a simple description: 'though to drive something away'. He may imagine it is a fly but we know that it is an unwelcome thought.

And now that thought comes out into the open, preceded by a graphic image of impending danger, that of a man walking calmly across a bridge over an abyss, only to realise half-way across that the bridge is broken and 'the abyss yawns below'. At this point, finally, he lets the thought he had been resisting all evening enter his consciousness: 'For the first time the probability of his wife's falling in love with anybody occurred to him, and he was horrified.' That 'horrified' [*uzhasnulsia*] is brilliant: it leaves open whether it horrifies him because he loves her or because of the interruption it might cause to the comfortable flow of his life and the damage it might do to his reputation.

That is enough for the moment. Just as Karenin needs to move in order to digest what he has only just allowed himself to think, so the reader needs to be returned to (apparently) simple description. For though Tolstoy seems to be merely describing Karenin's perambulation through the flat, the description of the rooms he walks through, the parquet of the dining-room, the carpet of the drawing-room, and especially the pictures hanging on the wall and the way they are lit, nudge us further into an understanding, more acute than Karenin's own, of the man, his background, and his assumptions. Most damning of course is the self-portrait on the wall, with the solitary light shining upon it, testifying to his sense of his own importance; but as he moves into his wife's sitting-room we also learn about her through the attention drawn to the portraits of her parents and friends on the walls and to the 'pretty little knick-knacks on her writing-table'. This world, hers within his, as it were, is clearly a source of comfort to her, but it also suggests the sense of imprisonment of which, like him, she is hardly aware.

But I suspect I have been insensitive to Tolstoy in describing him as 'nudging' the reader. What is so remarkable about Tolstoy is that we rarely have the sense, as we do in lesser writers, of any of this as having been planted so as to make the points the author wishes to make; rather, they form part of a whole which, we sense, arises in Tolstoy's imagination and which he has the skill to convey to us. To see them as planted is to read too suspiciously.

The novel deflects suspicion in many ways, but especially by taking into its orbit not only the story of Anna and her husband but also of her brother and his wife and of Kitty and Levin. The sections we are looking at are followed by the wonderful passages on Levin, who has retreated to his country estate to try to get over the pain of Kitty's rejection of his marriage proposal; and by the short section on the coming of spring in the countryside in particular, which takes us from individual human crises to the larger rhythms of nature, which is both oblivious to these things and at the same time and perhaps for precisely that reason, strangely consoling. That is what people mean when they talk of Tolstoy's epic style. Like Homer, who can describe a warrior falling from his chariot, pierced through with a javelin as like a diver leaping from a high rock into the sea, Tolstoy's art of narrative juxtaposition helps us to see individual lives within a larger whole.

And yet. Being where we are, with Proust and Kafka and Joyce and Woolf between us and Tolstoy, it is impossible not to see, if even for a moment, what I have

described as part of a whole as being one item after another planted there to further the author's purpose. We have in a sense been made bad readers of Tolstoy by what stands between him and us. We cannot help but think, at least on occasion, reading him, of the artist putting the construct together to persuade us of the truth of his vision rather than allowing ourselves to live unquestioningly in his world. This is something we never do with Homer, even though there are a great many more artists standing between him and us. Why is this?

In part I think it is because with Homer we are clearly in an oral world. The bard tells us from the outset that he is reliant for his story on the Muse and every line reminds us of this fact: the Muse (or the tradition) gives him his material and his form (fixed epithets, lines with their strict rhythmic rules, and so on) and he shapes it. Tolstoy, on the other hand, is an individual with a distinctive style and set of concerns. He is wonderful in the way his nature is, in his most successful works, like Shakespeare's, 'subdued / To what it works in, like the dyer's hand' (Sonnet 111). Yet the fact that we note this as an achievement suggests that it is a kind of overcoming, a kind of warding off.

What is it that is being overcome, warded off?

Background and Foreground

When Marcel Duchamp remarked in an interview that 'the imperative to paint in background is degrading for a painter' he was, as so often with him, articulating in a brief sentence what it would take a long disquisition to unpack. Essentially, he was questioning the nature of the art of the West with which he had grown up, an art that felt the need to persuade the viewer that what he or she was seeing enclosed within the frame was a faithful reproduction of something that already existed, whether a known historical episode, a story from mythology, a landscape or a figure. When the relations between the artist and his patron or market were unquestioned this was taken as natural, it was the kind of thing the patron wanted and the artist was there to produce it, for a fee. But once artists began to question the market and to ask what it was they were in effect doing, they began to feel that what they were making they were making in the first place not because they needed to earn their living but because it was something they wanted to do or felt called upon to do. What this was, of course, was not clear, but that it had to do with self-fulfilment, with what, in the case of a painter like van Gogh, could even be called a religious vocation, rather than with money or prestige was not in doubt. And with that came the sense that every stroke of the brush was significant and had in a sense to be accounted for. The consequence was the gradual disappearance in non-academic artists, of the dichotomy between background and foreground, whether in van Gogh or Cézanne, or in the parallel case of music, in Schoenberg or Varèse.

Nowhere is the development clearer yet nowhere is it more difficult to grasp than in the field of the novel. For background, in what we call the classic novel, is more than a question of setting, more, to return to Tolstoy, than the apartment through which Karenin walks in his anguished attempt to understand what it is that is happening to him and his marriage. It is Karenin himself and his life-story, Anna and her life-story, Levin and Kitty and Vronsky and Oblonsky and all that we learn about them, unobtrusively, from Tolstoy.

And not just what we learn about Oblonsky's sybaritic nature or Vronsky's relations to his regiment, but every detail, however tiny, however insignificant, however ephemeral, in the larger picture presented to us, and which helps Tolstoy build up his portrait of a failed marriage and its tragic consequences. Here, for example is a moment, one might say an insignificant moment, in the shoot undertaken one evening by Levin and Oblonsky, who has come to visit him at his estate in the country:

> In the thicket the birds chirped louder and more busily. Nearby a brown owl hooted, and Laska gave a start, took a few cautious steps, and, putting her head on one side, pricked up her ears again. A cuckoo was heard on the other side of the stream. It called twice on its usual note, and then gave a hoarse, hurried call and broke down.
>
> 'Fancy, the cuckoo already!' said Oblonsky, appearing from behind a bush. (180)

This is what we love Tolstoy for, his ability to encompass both Karenin's anguish *and* these two friends out shooting snipe on an early Spring evening. But, a Duchampian sceptic might ask, where did this owl come from, this cuckoo? The thicket, the birds, the dog – they have all been conjured up by Tolstoy in order to convey to us the feel of this moment. They are there to set the scene, to make us feel Levin's happy integration in his rural life, which is as real for him as his love for Kitty in St Petersburg, if not more so, just as Vronsky's passion for horses is as real if not more so than his love for Anna; and all this helps Tolstoy tell his story of Anna and Kitty and Karenin and Levin and Vronsky and Oblonsky. But, the Duchampian would say, am I condemned to invent all these details till the end of my working life?

But what is wrong with that? we might respond. And no doubt Duchamp would answer, Nothing, but it's not for me, I personally find it degrading to be asked to do it. And behind that 'I' is Duchamp's wager that it is he who speaks for the artist of his day, not those who would slavishly follow Tolstoy.

You do not ask what is the background of Bloom in *Ulysses* or Estragon in *Waiting for Godot* or Cinoc in Perec's *Life: A User's Manual*. You may be given it but it is quite likely to be contradicted elsewhere in the works in which they appear. Not because the writer is teasing us, but because *he doesn't know*. Or rather, if that answer is seen as too coy, because he could have chosen for it to be this or this or this or this and there is nothing to allow him to decide which. Any back story, such a writer feels, would inevitably be arbitrary, and therefore would inevitably have the stamp of a subjective choice by the author, which forces him to ask: Why should I pick one out and pretend it is true simply for the satisfaction of my reader? Have I really given up so much in my life, made the choice of spending hours every day writing

fiction, merely to satisfy my reader?

Listen to one Duchampian story-teller, Hamm in Beckett's *Endgame*: 'It was an extra-ordinarily bitter day, I remember, zero by the thermometer... It was a glorious day, I remember, fifty by the heliometer, but already the sun was sinking down into the... It was a howling wild day, I remember, a hundred by the anemometer. The wind was tearing up the dead pines... It was an exceedingly dry day, I remember, zero by the hygrometer. Ideal weather for my lumbago...' Each of these possibilities could be made plausible, *readable*, by Hamm. But he feels, as no doubt Beckett feels, that such story-telling is merely his way of keeping himself from facing the fact that 'you're on earth, there's no cure for that!'

In his late work Beckett grows more relaxed, less angry. But what drives his writing, both constrains and releases it, does not change. 'A voice comes to one in the dark. Imagine.' That is how *Company* begins. A voice, he soon explains/discovers 'devising it all for company.' The voice may tell him to imagine, and this will allow him to remember and so to produce his most serenely autobiographical work. Yet those memories or imaginings are licensed, so to speak, only by being anchored so firmly to a voice coming to one in the dark – and Beckett exploits with relish the fact that 'one' is both oneself and anyone.

Anna Karenina gives the impression that it is, somehow, writing itself. Tolstoy's mastery is seemingly so effortless that once – usually with the first sentence – we have entered this world we cease to think of it as a story and think of it as – what? In truth we don't think of it at all, we just read and allow the work to fill our imagination. Perhaps we should call it an unfolding, both an unfolding of the many lives we encounter in the course of the book and of our own sense of ourselves and our own possibilities. In this again it is like a Beethoven sonata or symphony. For contrary to what is often said, Beethoven's power over us comes not from the assertion of his mighty will, his overwhelming personality, but from the sense that it is not a piece of music that is unfolding before (and within) us but life itself, our own life in particular. You never feel this with Mozart or Haydn, with them there is always the sense of a *performance*, of something made and then remade in the concert hall for us each time we attend a concert. And the same is true of Bach and indeed of all music before Beethoven.

We might then say that the artists of the modern era I have been talking about go out of their way to remind us of what came naturally to Mozart and Haydn: that this is a construction, something made and remade as we watch, listen, read. But the modern work of art differs in one fundamental aspect both from its nineteenth-century predecessors and from the art of earlier times. It no longer feels natural to perform, it no longer seems required by society. And so for the modern artist filled with Duchampian scepticism there is something inherently absurd, inherently impossible about the whole enterprise.

And yet it is not enough to suggest a course of treatment for this scepticism, or to point to their contemporaries who do not seem infected by it. For, to them – and, believe me, they have looked – there is no treatment available and what they feel about their uninfected contemporaries is that their work is in a strange way hollow, unreal. They seem to be like that pseudo-swimmer Kierkegaard talks about, who hung himself from the ceiling in a harness and moved his arms and legs vigorously and imagined he was swimming.

Can we decide who is right here?

Full and Empty Speech

There is a fascinating letter by Paul Celan in which he insists that reality for the poem is in no way something fixed, predetermined, but something that is at issue, something to be questioned. He returns to this in his lecture, *The Meridian*: the poem does not describe, he says here, it is an exploration, an activity. And we feel this as we read Proust or Woolf or Beckett, that the work is not the transcription of a story which the author is telling us but rather is itself a movement of discovery. The philosopher John Mepham explains this in a fine essay on Woolf's *To the Lighthouse*. 'The traditional novel,' he writes, 'is a form of representation which involves the creation of an imaginary but well-ordered fictional space. Within this space are represented the relationships, the dramas and the destinies of individual lives.' 'Well-ordered' is the key here, for though the story may involve apparently confused and chaotic accidents and the depiction of crises in the lives of the characters which they often do not comprehend it is a precondition of the novel that the narrator is immune to this (that is why *Tristram Shandy*, written in the 1750s, in which this axiom is under assault from the very beginning, feels such a modern work, so out of place in its time).

'But what,' asks Mepham, 'if we lack this sense of epistemological security? What if our experience seems fragmented, partial, incomplete, disordered? Then writing might be a way not of representing but of creating order.' 'Think,' he says, 'about the memory one might have of a person one has loved.' It is rare that our feelings in this instance are clear and orderly. Rather,

> we might have the feeling that the remembered person escapes us, is ungraspable, cannot be contained in our minds except as a disordered flow of particular fragments of memory of some particular scenes, some images, gestures, a tone of voice, haunting phrases, perhaps particularly significant colours and sounds... Then we would feel... that there was something to be said but that we lacked the means of saying it.

In that case, he says:

> Narration would not be the embodiment of some pre-existing knowledge, but the satisfaction of the desire to speak with appropriate intensity about things of which our knowledge is most uncertain.

Mepham's remarks remind me not of traditional criticism but rather of certain modern trends in psychoanalysis, and especially of Lacan and his school. A recent essay on Perec and psychoanalysis makes the point well:

> Psychoanalysis is not straightforwardly the talking cure in the sense of a cure by talking. It is also, equally, perhaps even more important, the cure for talking – for a certain kind of talking that Lacan called 'empty speech', a form of speech he distinguished from its opposite, full speech. He defined full speech as follows: 'Full speech is speech which aims at, which forms, the truth such as it becomes established in the recognition of one person by another. Full speech is speech which performs.' (Roger Bacon, Georges Perec, W, and the making of *The Memory of Childhood*', *Raritan*, Fall 2020, pp.92–118)

The reason for what Beckett described as *cacoethes scribendi*, the mania for writing (Greek *kakos*, bad, + *ethos*, innate tendency) of writing, and whose hold over him he never ceased to lament, is simple: it is the desire to achieve that 'full speech' of which Lacan speaks. But unlike the psychoanalysts, who, in their more optimistic moments, imagine that a successful cure, meaning the finding of such speech, is possible (Freud was more realistic or pessimistic at the end of his life in talking of 'Psycho-analysis Terminable and Interminable'), the writers, in particular Kafka and Beckett, seem to feel that while writing can lead towards such speech it will also, inevitably, fall short of it.

What neither Kafka nor Beckett can say, but what we feel, reading them, is that the struggle to achieve a full speech itself leads, if not to fullness of speech, then at least away from the failures of a facile and empty speech, and that that, for us humans, is enough – though for someone like Virginia Woolf, Celan or Berryman, it was, alas, in the end, not enough.

To the Lighthouse is a particularly apposite example of course, because, as Virginia Woolf herself acknowledged, the book is her attempt to bring to life, *for her*, her long dead mother. But Mepham's remarks apply to all the modern works I have been talking about. Of course there is a sense in which even so well-ordered and controlled a work as *Anna Karenina*, like any great work of art, is only written because its author will not fully understand what it is he wants to say till he has written it. But the differences are nevertheless profound. So profound that we may well feel they inhabit different universes.

Reading and Writing

There are times, when I am tired or unhappy, when only the Tolstoy and Dickens mode of story-telling will help me, only works where I can forget myself in the creations of the author. I go to them precisely because they lack the self-consciousness of their modern counterparts or *their* precursors. On the other hand there are times when Tolstoy and Dickens feel lifeless, fossils of a bygone age, when only *Tristram Shandy* or Kafka will satisfy me. Only they, I feel at such times, will quicken me, remind me of what is important in life and of what art can do.

The differences are even more marked when it is a question of my own writing. What a reasoned account of the differences between the 'classical' and the modern, such as I hope I have given, misses, is the violence and pain behind Duchamp's remark that it is degrading for the artist to be asked to fill in the background. For example, when I write down: 'It was a warm spring evening and the moon was out', my whole body cries out against it. To stand by it would, I feel at such times, be a betrayal, a denial akin to Peter's of Christ in the Gospels. Similarly, if I were to write about a man who feels that he suddenly sees into his wife's soul, and notes 'that the depths of her soul, always open to him, were now closed against him', the one sentence I could never write is precisely this one. The excitement of writing the book would lie, for me, in conveying this without ever saying it.

The prohibition is the spur. Only that which asks to be said but for which there are no words will generate new work that is genuine and therefore good. Peter Handke, in his moving account of his mother, *A Sorrow Beyond Dreams*, puts it like this: 'The utmost need to communicate goes to hand in hand with the ultimate speechlessness.' But it is Emily Dickinson who puts it best of all:

> In many and reportless places
> We feel a Joy –
> Reportless, also, but sincere as Nature
> Or Deity –
>
> It comes, without a consternation –
> Dissolves – the same –
> But leaves a sumptuous Destitution –
> Without a Name –
>
> Profane it by a search – we cannot
> It has no home –
> Nor we who having once inhaled it –
> Thereafter roam.

Five Poems

BILL MANHIRE

Angry Man

He has three barking dogs in the back of the car,
old Silas and... I don't know the others.
He has parked the car up over the kerb outside the library
and is standing nearby, waiting to see what will happen.

But nothing happens. He stands there all day
and the dogs fall asleep, and he opens the car door
and now the moon and stars are out in the sky
and here is the light by which his children read their books.

Library Song

The man from the Ministry of Health
has placed my books upon his shelf.
Sometimes he takes one down for me
if I sit where he can see.

He does not read books much himself.

This is a happy time,
especially when the day clouds over.
I hold the book all day, all day,
until the time for reading's over.

His name is Mr Crimson
though the colour of his heart is gray.
I ask him if it is true about his heart
but he says he has not looked and so he cannot say.

He says, The time for reading is over
for the daylight is nearly gone.
This book must now return
to the shelf it rests upon.

The man from the Ministry of Health
has taken my book from me.
He has placed it on the high shelf carefully
with all the other books he has taken away from me.

Pioneer

We need to ford the river.
There's always the other side to consider.
Whether we think about the other side or not,
we need to ford the river.

The boats go on the river
and the river goes on forever.
We need somewhere to come ashore,
a somewhere we haven't been before.

Look over there! A giant flightless bird!
A tree shaped like a pear!
Do we feel fear? We don't. We do?
You know I'll never agree with you.

We like to think we're starting to explore
deep into the far and furthermore.
We use words like hitherto a lot,
we sit by the campfire, watch the clock.

Yet even with the heat, we start to shiver.
We really need to talk.
So many things on which we differ!
When to say whence, when to say whither.

But first of all we need to ford the river.

Yawn

His name was Yawn and he came from Iceland.
He started talking about glaciers.
I said, well we have those.
Then it was thermal stuff and bubbling mud.
All that, too, I said. Volcanoes. Ditto.
Waterfalls. Of course.

Then he said, we have no trees, another interesting fact.
We have lots of those, I said. Big forests. Bush.
He said, I don't think you can even see
where you are going with all those trees.

Then he turned on his heel
and vanished into the polar wastes.

Maybe it was Yone, but I will stick with Yawn.
I called after him, words I am still quite proud of:
Well, you can't beat a good diorama!
Whenever I fall asleep, I think of him.

At Lake Dickinson

This landscape needs a better sky,
something to look the water in the eye.

A single cloud would do,
should you have one on or about you.

How Does This Look?

KIRSTY GUNN

I watch my daughters getting ready to go out and it occurs to me how – though we don't talk about them much, in ordinary life, I mean – adjectives make up a huge part of who we are. 'Lovely,' I say to the girls, as they pile on some glamorous top or other, change their shoes for the third time. 'Gorgeous.' These kinds of words spring out of my mouth on a pretty regular basis – the perfects, the wonderfuls – but are they really even descriptions? Adumbrations? Ornamentation, even? 'Beautiful.' I say, just like everyone does in *The Awkward Age*, that novel by Henry James which is about the kind of society that is not beautiful at all. I may only mean 'beautiful' to be beautiful when I say it but by contrast Henry James is acutely aware in each of his books how a description can operate to bring about pretty much any kind of outcome. James knows about adjectives, alright. He's alert not only to the sheer joy of putting them to use – setting a 'canicular' here, a delicately 'precipitate' or thumping great 'superimcumbent' there, to fill sentence after sentence with the kinds of multisyllabics that so coil and rumble as to set each off on a charged path towards high drama or comedy. But he also has the fun of employing them in the more usual sense of acting as a one word description, to light up the most ordinary thing. For why say basement flat in *The Ambassadors* when you could describe it as 'entresol' and 'innermost nook'? Or, in that same novel, attend to a gentleman's regular morning's shave when the blade, instead, can be made to come in contact with a 'matitutinal chin'? On top of all that, he also understands, this master of the metonym, how adjectives can be turned inside out to elevate or debase, applied in quite specific and pointed ways so that a lovely term rearranged around its subject may come to have a quite different effect. I use an adjective and it means no more than a maternal thumbs up before the two lassies waft out the door. James takes on the same word and it becomes the most devastating way to sum up venality and selfishness and a form of socially sanctioned sex trafficking and prostitution.

Whew! Who would have thought an adjective could be so... well, adjectival?

In *The Awkward Age*, entire situations and scenarios are 'beautiful', ideas and plots working out to nefarious ends, but, on the whole, what I'm coming to see is that it's the women in James' novels who are in receipt of most of the adjectives in them, the really good ones I mean. Julia walks in the door in *The Tragic Muse* in an amazing hat – 'Julia had come' – and, my goodness, there she is. Women take adjectives in the way James has them take them, to wear them, to show them off, in order to let themselves be seen. They need to be so accessorised – as well as wearing extraordinary hats, something she might touch lightly to adjust here and there, Julia has 'hair of so dark a brown... and so abundant that a plain arrangement was required to keep it in natural relation to the rest of her person' – in order to fit them for playing their large and important roles; their descriptions must dominate. More than is the case for the male protagonists in most of the novels, adjectives are applied to women and girls in such a way that place them firmly and correctively in a moral and social universe. Right from the outset the details we are given about Julia Dallow establish the kind of powerhouse she is, with her 'off hand cursory manner' and 'mouth like a rare pink flower'. We *get* her, her 'resolution and temper' and her beauty – and all in one go. The adjectives have hit the spot. Mrs Gereth slides up on to bench next to Fleda Vetch at the beginning of *The Spoils of Poynton* and it's the same sort of thing applied to a very different type. So much packed in. So much judgment and thought. Fearing her son's taste in women, 'that Owen would, in spite of all her spells, marry a frump', someone just 'tiresomely lovely' (for, as far as she is concerned, both terms are interchangeable) she sees by contrast in Fleda, 'one, slim, pale and black haired', 'dressed in thought'. In a couple of sentences the two women's characters are fixed: 'their eyes met and and sent out mutual soundings' in a world that seems vulgar and uncertain. Both matron and girl join forces in being mean about 'the abnormal nature of the Brigstocks', the family at whose home they are staying and 'from whose composition the principle of taste had been extravagantly omitted'. Fleda observes that the older woman 'was one of those who impose themselves as an influence' and that she has 'large, masterful white hands'. Descriptions of men do also *show* in various kinds of fashion, in James's pages, of course they do, but on the whole don't quite *tell* as much. Here's Mrs Gereth again, whose taste has been achieved with 'a patience, an almost infernal cunning'. She talks about her expensive furnishings all the time because she has accumulated them with 'a limited command of money'. It's why we see her principally in terms of those hands of hers and the stuff they handle – her tapestries and cups and bibelots and brocades. These things are who she is; they're all she is. 'There wouldn't have been money enough for anyone else, she said with pride.' Yes, her son Owen is important enough in this story, but all we really know of him, by contrast, is that he's 'handsome'. Fleda even thinks for a while he may be a bit dim. Men get to play the full spectrum in the books, ranging from creep to sweetheart, from Osmond Gilbert to Rowland Mallett, but while it may take a while to get to know what, say, Basil Ransom is up to in *The Bostonians* – despite his introductory description of someone 'dark, deep and glowing' – don't we just understand from the outset what his cousin is all about! Adjectives *turn* on the women in James' books, they are as a kind of lighting upon them, a special effect. We see right from the beginning of *The Bostonians* how description makes these people who they are. Olive comes into the room to meet Basil and she is all 'plain dark dress, without any ornament, and her smooth colourless hair was constrained' – and how she commands our attention, this 'pale girl with her light green eyes' who sits upon the sofa with her beautiful posture and long straight back as though for a sitting. She's a Sargeant portrait for a Boston drawing room, every bit as beautiful though stuck nevertheless in that painted pose within some heavy gilded frame. Basil by contrast, despite being told of his stature and height, is hard for us to see. A dark haired Mississippian who speaks with a Southern drawl, he's all slip and lounge. James lingers on Ransom's speaking – 'It is not in my power to reproduce by any combination of characters this charming dialect' he writes – because speaking turns out to be what Basil's all about. There's little in him of Olive's painted-in solidity, he lacks matter, and he can't understand her 'morbid' upright stance. There she is, a picture of probity and righteousness – and who is he? This person who speaks so much and only seems to come in and out of rooms? He's a man, with all his fancy talk – but what does he represent? What's his composition? It's going to take some time to discover how he'll work the plot to his advantage; it's going to take a lot of conversation and dialogue.

So it is that while men, on the whole, may do most of the talking in novels by Henry James, still it's the women, fully shown and presented to them, who hit the green button that says 'Go'! Olive walking into the room is when that novel begins. Isabel Archer, seen standing in the doorway in *The Portrait of the Lady*, is painted right there before us, a 'a tall girl in a black dress, bareheaded, as if she were staying in the house...' James writes. Of course these kinds of ideas are all developed and complicated as the novels go on – and of course, too, a female character may be given, from the get-go as an American reader might say, as much spirited dialogue as her male counterpart – Olive's testy responses to her cousin's drawl are a good example, and I've always happened to love the way Isabel Archer makes her first impression on a potential suitor by talking intimately and, some might say, at length with a little dog. But more than anything it's how she looks – Olive's shock stillness, Julia's feathery touch to her hat, Isabel's bare-headed height – key details kicking in before any tracts of dialogue are laid down, that put a woman in the centre of our attention and set the tone for the tale ahead. In fact, you might say, James' female characters begin with their adjectives. They start life as a synecdoche.

So Milly Theale and Miriam Rooth and Fernanda Brookenham enter upon the scene and everything follows from there – volition and action, the eventual set of a moral compass, final outcome and consequence all unspooling from that first glimpse. There's 'little Nanda', encountered first in *The Awkward Age* through her portrait 'in glazed white wood', the very image of her grandmother who was a great beauty and social figurehead, and nothing 'little' about her at all, of course, as even the men will come to see, for this is a novel full of inversion and if beautiful is not beautiful then little can only mean large. Eventually and naturally, according to James's unhurried rhythmic prose, how a woman looks will be overtaken by what she's doing, what she's done, and what she really wants to do – indeed these forces will come to be understood as working at the very centre of most of the novels. I've learned to see, through the prism of this author's attention, that while his plots turn around what people want or think they want, still, each starts with a someone who is captured precisely in a viewfinder made – for a writer who used so many of them – of just a few words.

Here's a lady, at the start of *The Europeans*, who 'gave a pinch to her waist with her two hands, or raised these members – they were very plump and pretty – to the multifold braids of her hair...' So does the author introduce us to the Baroness Munster, that socially mobile representative of a certain impoverished type whom James describes in another novel as being like 'velvet stretched too thin'. At the mirror her face 'forgot its melancholy' but, when she is not looked upon, how that same face 'began to proclaim that she was a very ill-pleased woman'. Is there something about adjective placement – here, that sinister 'multifold' hairdo – which might influence plot? The way a reduced and concentrated description will have consequence for the rest of the story? And might there be something presciently Jamesian going on here, educating us in point of view and presentation, that has a significance that reaches far beyond the novels' stage walls? For my part, I'm starting to realise that for all the talk of male gaze that rages around the subject of female characters in canonical fiction, and around the subject of women in general in the world, I've barely given thought until reading and re-reading Henry James novels as to how very much an author's key siting of a word might have to do with moral outcome. How that word 'characterisation' – so beloved of prose writers, an entire approach to writing a person on the page that bundles up descriptions and summaries and is added to and adjusted as the story goes on – may not be nearly as significant as the particular pinning of one quite specific broad brimmed hat – or set of plaits – to a head. I am even wondering if the idea of the thoughtfully condensed description of a female subject in a novel might come to figure as powerfully (for me at least!) as all my rudimentary understanding of feminist history and narrative when it comes to thinking about – to borrow a phrase from Adrienne Rich – the politics of what happens when a woman walks into a room.

For how what is described – as detail, as colour, as accessory – becomes what is! It's something to think about as I send my daughters out the door. How the fact of the sentence 'Charlotte Stant, the next minute, was with them' in the opening section of *The Golden Bowl* combines with the impression she makes in that minute, 'in all her person, in motion and gesture, in free, vivid, yet happy altogether indications of dress', 'of not being afraid.' Those words, 'free', 'vivid', will come to describe, more than any amount of long form 'characterisation', that woman's ranging ambition and concupiscence. Charlotte's person takes off, of course, and goes from strength to strength, her knowing and getting (nearly) exactly what she wants. But how can she not be anyone other than who she is when we first meet her as having about her 'exactly the look of her adventurous situation'? In the same way, Maggie Verver, her lover's quiet wife who is described by him in the simple terms of apparent praise that only mark indifference – 'young, good, generous' – will show that very quality of her quietness to have a mighty strength. There's a hint of it early on when Charlotte appears with a parasol and hat which announces, in James's words, a most 'definite intention'. Both words, 'definite' and 'adventurous'... They have been fixed in our minds from the start and will have outcomes to match. There are consequences for such adjectives; they lead the way. So what exactly might be parsed, then, I find myself wondering, from my sort of response to a young girl's turn of shoe or colour of coat? Is a 'lovely' really quite enough? Responsible, even? What might be my alternative first thought/ best thought that would carry within it the kind of complicated and nuanced meaning James's adjectives carry, for my daughters to take out into society and to all their friends and then *use?* How might an adjective – I guess I am asking – help them *be?*

That from the very beginning of an interaction a description might be fixed in the heart and head, used to sound a base note, as it were, lay out the ground upon which to stand... This is a compelling idea to arise from a back-to-back reading of Henry James. Yes, there are occasions when it may take a while for his lens to finally focus upon its central subject – and just think about the number of pages until we finally get to clap eyes on the reason for Chad Newsome's delay in Paris, for example, in *The Ambassadors* – but when it does... Well *Goodness!*, as the plainly dressed and plain speaking Sarah Pocock in that novel might say. Haven't we realised now why that young man has so tarried? It's precisely because Madame de Vionnet couldn't be seen properly up until then, was not described, that poor Lambert Strether didn't know what he was up against. We only meet her, through him, finally, just over a third of the way through *The Ambassadors* – page 135 of 393 in my old Penguin edition – and even then we still can't really get a good look at her. 'She was dressed in black but in a black that struck him as light and transparent.' What? What kind of black dress? It's near impossible to visualise and only flashes light. And then a follow up impression is formed where the same woman is now 'showy and uncovered'... So altogether she's a shape shifter, this one, 'muffled one day... uncovered the next'. Fifty pages later, in the shadowy interior of Notre Dame, we meet her again – but again, there's something receding about her, hard to catch. This is James working his inversion of description again: 'he suddenly measured the suggestive effect of a lady' he writes, who 'wasn't prostrate – not in any degree bowed', who seems in the shadowy distance but then he 'happened to feel that someone, unnoticed, had approached him and paused.' How in our not seeing here, we also come to see. Someone barely present; and there's something awful going on here – though we can't put our finger on why exactly we think so. We can't *encompass* Madame de Vionnet by our seeing, anymore than Strether can. He realises 'She was the lurking figure of the dim chapel', is conscious of the way her impression has been made upon him, 'the way her slightly thicker veil was drawn... the composed gravity of her dress... the quiet of her folded, grey gloved hands.' But

this shade, this 'lurking' creature enclosed in the habit of 'one of the old women' of Notre Dame, is a thing in camouflage, placed away over there in a dark corner of the stone cathedral. In a rustle of 'subdued' dress, like the movement of air, she eludes Strether's physical vision and takes up place, like the devil, within his soul, Who could have guessed a veiled supplicant in such nondescript dress could be the blazing centre of a novel about female power? Yet James's adjectives have been working away counter-intuitively – quietly and modestly – towards exactly that conflagration. 'Veiled', 'old', 'grey'... The very words which have seemed to efface Madame de Vionnet set her alight.

The irresistible charm of certain women – and James is interested in the type, for sure, good and bad, his books are full of Princess Casamassimas and Mrs Assinghams and Kate Croy and Madame Merle, all creatures around or for whose ends the world and the people in it, rotate and fall – is lost only on another kind of woman who also features large, a formidable opponent to them. Sarah Pocock, in *The Ambassadors*, is like Mrs Touchett and Doctor Prance in other novels, bracingly opinionated, clear thinking and sensible, taking no nonsense from anything satin or veiled, grey or otherwise. They see through disguises, these women who wear mackintoshes and trousers, and have no truck with parasol points such as those artfully employed by people like Maisie's mother and Gertrude's cousin. Doctor Prance, in *The Bostonians*, always sensibly dressed, sums up in an instant the cod feminism that's been touted by Verena Tarrant's entourage. 'She's practising her speech' is the way she describes Verena's preparations for that character's great spiritual outpouring of female truth and vision. And Doctor Prance herself, though she does show a 'Mephistophelean gleam of a smile', really needs only her pair of trousers to indicate how clever she is. How she does stand apart – excepting for a residual loyalty to an old suffragette stalwart who goes by the highly descriptive name of Miss Birdseye – from the uncertainty and dilly dallying of the other characters who fill up the rest of this book. Who wants to be described anyway? such a character may be suggesting. Who wants to have their sensibility and emotional landscape writ large in words that are only about seeing and looking? 'I have that within which passeth show' says Hamlet, and I like to remind my daughters of that idea from time to time. You look lovely as you are, I say – but also it really doesn't matter. It's only a dress. Life need not be about what is seen in the mirror, I might remind them – though the mirror draws young girls towards it, I know, and is there for all of us, whether we like it or not.

Because, as James and Shakespeare both tell us, appearance does count – as a 'show' of who we are, and who we *want* to be. And that 'passeth' has multiple meanings, of course. Hamlet may be more complex than he seems, but he also wants to pass as a regular guy; and that no one will know what he's really thinking is what he's after, too. He wants to pass off as being someone else in that way, or pass altogether, so nobody will notice him even, that he might be lucky enough to be totally ignored. Showing, telling. Letting the one turn into the other, and back again... James's adjectives work the same alchemy. From the 'light' that shines from Fleda in *The Spoils* to the 'so little superstitiously in the fashion' black silk that shrouds Milly in *The Wings of the Dove*, from the 'frazzled' to the 'gleaming'. This one, 'presumptive', that one, 'effaced', invisible, nearly. Placed just so, a word, at an exact point in the sentence, or here, right here, at another... Each simile, each metaphor and detail has made me consider the precise role this part of speech plays in our social, communal life. Out the door and onto the stage of the world swish my two girls and my poor reaction has operated as no kind of description of how they may seem in that production. Yet description matters; it can help us as clearly as it can distract, and Henry James has made me think about how adjectives are a way of thinking about others – people we know and love, along with strangers – as well as a literary term applied to our writing and reading of books. For what does it mean to describe someone, and describe them exactly? In life and in a novel? Though poets might think about adjectives all the time, what do novelists need to consider when bringing a person (or a place, for that matter, but place is not my subject here) into the world of our pages? I am thinking, I guess, as much about a poetics of prosopography as to the ethics of description, here – the terrible and wonderful power we have when we describe one person to another. How secretly and cleverly and cunningly and also lovingly and generously we might elevate or debase.

As I've written before in these pages,* Henry James's prose can lead the mind towards this kind of – what we prose writers might call – poetry thinking: How one sees his crafting of a sentence bearing all the marks of a piece of language that is as ornately articulated as a sonnet. And now that I've been looking in the way I have at the women in these novels of his, and how they are presented, I've come to be more aware, not only of what adjectives can do, but what they might do *to* us – how they contain within them effect *and* affect, both, giving us an awareness of the heightened thing and the thing itself in the raw that stands behind it. So there's the glazed

and lovely finish of paint that is the portrait of Miriam Rooth in *The Tragic Muse*, and there too, the vulgar, rough voiced ingenue who is still contained somewhere within the body of the actress who sat for it. We meet her first, as one of an odd pair of 'strange women'; James writes of an old character in 'an ancient, well used shawl' and someone else. 'The other person was very much younger', we read, 'and had a pale face, a low forehead and thick dark hair...' How that low forehead does come forward, and stays with us – despite the 'largely gazing eyes' also present in our line of vision. This one, that one, indeed.

So, in the end, they might do a double job, these adjectives of ours. Lie as well as tell the truth. Represent desire as well as its dissolve. They show the shine on a thing that, the moment it is highlighted, fades. They describe the expectation that comes with talking up a noun, and the end of expectation once that job's been done – the awful realisation that there's no more of an experience to come. So they might be, these 'describing words' as we teach children to call them, both attempt at and limitation of expression – for even when they come off (and a perfectly placed adjective can come off, in life, as in a Henry James novel, in very wonderful ways indeed) still, don't they leave us curiously... wanting? I see it in my daughters' faces in the mirror: Yes, that will do very nicely but is that *all*? The outfit? The jacket? No ornament, no addition, no word, ends up being quite good enough. Or, in another scenario, the description has taken over completely. So there's the dress, say, but where's the girl? Henry James has made me pay attention to all this... And more. Who or what exactly is being looked at in that mirror? There's Julia again 'lifting her hands for some re-arrangement of her hat', 'her fine head poised' and reflected back at us. And we start reading in order to learn to see.

* See PNR 258, recommending a thorough, immersive reading of the novels of Henry James as a literary practice not unlike learning to play the piano.

Three Poems

JAY GAO

Hostis

take care, do not know me,
deny me, do not recognise me,

shun me; for this reality
is infectious
— H.D.

Flying home, west, I hitch my pity
onto the mosquito trapped under the cling film
of this exotic dragon fruit salad. On its last long leg we shared
one vessel. Its authority to inflict human suffering unsettled me,
as I carefully ate around the heritages housing its stuck body.
I had read an article that said our kinship with them
can be most compellingly imagined through the metaphor of war.
You have killed nearly half of all the humans
that have ever lived; there is little of history left over you have not
yet touched. And so, the article explained, even expatriate mosquitoes
will, one day, clandestinely evolve some resistance to their poison,
artemisinin, with each new generation. Unless we modify
the fertility genes in the females; eradicate, in an entire genus,
the vector for disease. Genius
and victory. I have just watched the final scene from *In the Mood*
for Love again. I cried again.
I fled a similar unpicked itch.
Those strangler figs in Angkor Wat cosset a stonier intimacy
better left tongue-tied in the flesh. I wanted to be back on that buried
path towards enlightenment. Try again
the inauthentic itinerary for touring a mountain home for the gods.
Pavilion Indochine Hotel. Tick. Your prophylactic regimen. Tick.
Rain as warm as blood. Tick. And my hired driver for the day,
not much older than me,
chain-smoked American cigarettes, texted his boyfriend,
blared Khmer pop from his tuk-tuk camouflaged in Coca-Cola
logos. Later, left alone in a Lucky Burger, probing
the meaty dregs of a mango smoothie with a straw,
I felt like such a nobody. And how I loved that bad air. How
did it feel to have just conquered a world wonder? Plundered
it with the lens of a dirty phone assembled in Shenzhen, China.
Even the foreign ear of a guest cupped
against a wall can rob stone of all its kissing music.
The photographs of statues I kept near to my wallet like a deck
of lethal military technologies. Headless men
filled to their necks with stagnant water. Yet the mosquito and I,
we both consented to lengthen our link a little longer.
Inside our cabin ecosystem,
perfectly calibrated so that host rules reign supreme,
homesickness infects us both.
Nostalgic, I smuggle the mosquito in an old scar
behind my right ear, and listen, from its blurry world below,
for the wet choral buzzing of larva who curve
their sleep beyond muddy colonies: might they dream
of more classic things, of past lives lived out in a touched
and looted and ruinous state.

Hero Worship

I wake to stay in bed again, decide
every minor error of mine will remain broken in its wildness.
Nights of loss now end peacefully and rarely with restless
sediment. Beyond doubt, I no longer feel alone.
Update on security incident is the subject of these siren emails;
so it seems ghosts keep trying to hack the university's global
trade routes. I dream about our sacred technicians haunting around
the anxious clock. Deep breathing. Remain
vigilant. I remind myself I am the translation machine. Excavated,
I am multiplying. In the morning, it must have snowed
even if I did not witness it.
This inert world seemed so buried with an off-white energy
yet to be exploited, and I made a gambit to get my body out of there,
a homecoming in disguise, my old return. Jupiter, Saturn,
Mercury aligned a few weeks ago without me even knowing.
Yet I could still perceive it. I think I slept right through it,
like a dress rehearsal before death.
No matter how many rooms
I gift my heroic molecules, they refuse to fall in line,
to deterritorialise. I will be honest, I am excited to know what aporias
you will be planning soon, I praise our tenantless sun.
This year, I resolve to be both at home and not,
wet with words, my fingers within language
then doing without.
One childhood ambition was to project myself way into the past,
to be consoled only by classical bodies.
I always wanted to end by walking backwards, trace
slower circles in my back garden; in the distance,
beyond the steel mountains, I hear a train slip back into
the platform of its avant-garde station with a click, that snap of setting
a pen's cap back on. The hands of the train are lifted
straight up as if to say: O.K. You got me. I admit it,
I yield my tempo. So just let me surrender
over all my worlded goods to you.

Imperium Abecedarian

Oh! Adventurer
Oh! Boss
Oh! Coloniser
Oh! Despot
Oh! Emperor
Oh! Fascist
Oh! God
Oh! Hero
Oh! Imperator
Oh! Jailer
Oh! King
Oh! Leader
Oh! Monarch
Oh! Nazi
Oh! Overlord
Oh! Pioneer
Oh! Queen
Oh! Ruler
Oh! Sovereign
Oh! Translator
Oh! Usurper
Oh! Voyeur
Oh! Wanderer
Oh! Xénos
Oh! You
Oh! Zealot

let us start the clock

Six Poems

LOUIS KLEE

Some Output of Beauty

Humiliating beauty
black white fire burning in books
I sit outside your window, I
make my outhouse by your house

Walled in by windows
guesthouse for the wind
hovel among cucumbers
I am not unhappy

Nightly wood dark comes
in blue, wind-thinned
clouds in the shallow valley
you fire up the lamps

Shut in my salt cellar, I
peer in at your splendour
from where it's dark
what you see out

Me by Louis Fratino

Dirigible I felt your pampered roundness
grow around me as though I were seeds
soft within fruit – oh, everything!
Someone made this
for us:
coffee and eggs, Mario Mieli
somewhere wrote this, lemon and splendid
rugs and pink to tint with
acid-mauve for flecked hints
so we could do modernism as we pleased
again and again, in mood
for preludes to the world's musk
blue like the powder that clings to bodies
washing my knees in summer light in red
abstraction when I walked the city
between break ups and found everyone
was gentle with me, except the one I love.

Never Any End to Blue

They will make the poem out of birch wood
and it will be three lines by four
and loose enough to remain permeable to the stronger
wind and rain, and allow for the forceful sort
of gorgeousness that would impress itself anyhow.
Though not so slack as to house this madness in the work.
They will paint it in sky blue or a muted tone of pink
or, if need be, the lemon blue now fashionable,
for there is never any end to blue –
what might already be quite useless
what I'm concerned with here, something else – say
who fashions thinly for chinks, who will see the larger stars.

'There are other poems'

There are other poems.
This is a vision of a village in rain.
The inconsequence, the incursion of a good storm
and birds at outlandish vantage, rivers
and sea, and every kind of tree, the stars
and many more such things you find in poems:
boot slurring in clay where the car slipped
a small ditch and there the coiled swan, she is
still clambering to warm a still born egg,
instinct maybe, unlasping from a barge
of rotting leaves. This England or shingle
spit left-over of Doggerland where I do my tenancy
No exile, poet, you are a tenant, small
body for all this world by the lake again
in late summer we found a pocked
pebble, comet that had consummated itself
in our atmosphere and rested by me
as softly as ready fruit.

Counter-Song

When I read this poem to my mother
she said luckless boy – you always did
like bark.

Bird built

with mud and spit. No other god now
but you and you shrug and say love,
child of plenty and poverty, lapsed
symmetry, his boyfriend, his clipped
betterment for fervourance: strive,
strive away at night our walls, the dust
lurches strange, and it falls.
The breast can press it, lint it,
the body bare in a copse how birds
collapse toward you from sky. Hail
then bright, then hail and more
thens, many, the sheer move of them.
Let it. Walls will manner, it's night.
At the flip of a shred, we hold curves now
with flight but to how. No cause. To risk
being understood, apparently, and racked
with pleasure commit some walk
out to how when so much sheerly
might just be not yet

Other Tongues: Logos & Eros

IAIN BAMFORTH

Advice for the deaf

It is simply profounder, the poet Gottfried Benn writes in his considered essay on old age, to suffer the human lot in *silence*. A statement like that looks suspicious coming from a writer whose collected works fill several thousand pages in the Klett-Cotta edition. The same applies to Pascal Quignard who, at the latest count, has published over eighty titles. He says of himself in an interview, 'Et plutôt que porte-parole, je me sens porte-silence'. If he isn't a spokesman then, he must be a rather peculiar kind of quietist.

Without language how would we ever know that suffering in silence is meaningful *at all*, as these writers claim? What both writers are hinting at, I think, is that the very act of speaking (not to mention writing) opens the deconstructive possibility of irony.

The true master says nothing, his readers being his living intentions.

Phenomenology of the jawbone

The higher, robotic 'iron angel' lifeforms that will ultimately be destroyed by rust and mould in Stanislaw Lem's story 'The White Death' observe the gross custom exhibited by members of the species among which they find themselves stranded: these repellent organic lifeforms keep stuffing various other objects into the back of their face. It is not known why they do this, whether it is some kind of destructive ritual or a method for draining off venom or a brute manifestation of greed, 'for [they] would consume everything if they were able'.

The robots are of course observing human eating behaviour. And what these organic lifeforms are doing is, as we have guessed, all three – insofar as eating is the incorporation of knowledge into bodily substance. *Genesis* starts with a story about eating because like other mammalian species it is our fate to have to tear the substance of other living things apart in our mouths while using the same orifice to create the variety of sounds, intimate and public, that we call language. The self-image of our own nobility as the unique 'language animal' was always going to be compromised by the nature of the base needs passing through the same mouth. As Samuel Butler put it, 'Eating is touch carried to the bitter end'. The mineral solidity of teeth gives them a terrifying quality. And as if biting, grinding and chewing weren't daunting enough, we then have to swallow what we eat. Swallowing is the mechanism which allows for the prehension of foodstuffs and prepares them, already partly broken down and pre-digested, as a bolus to be propelled towards the acid bath of the stomach while ensuring that the airways remain protected. And while phonation might be the least important laryngeal function in terms of brute survival, it is certainly the most expressively 'human' function.

Even then, for some observers, speaking can seem as gross a custom as eating. This is the narrator's conclusion in Céline's novel *Voyage au bout de la nuit*: 'When you spare a thought for how words are shaped and spoken, our sentences hardly stand up to the disaster of their slobbery origins.'

Little wonder, then, that in some Gnostic tracts, the intestinal tract is regarded as the refuge of the serpent of the first chapters of *Genesis*, the snake somehow having wound its way into the Adamic anatomy there to be transformed into a hollow tube. And why Jesus, in one of his parables (Matthew 15:11), attempts to reverse the ethics of consumptive thinking: 'Not that which goeth into the mouth defileth a man; but that which cometh out of the mouth, this defileth a man.'

This was hardly a revolutionary observation: already *Proverbs* had recommended the ways of discretion and reticence. As the popular saying has it: a closed mouth collects no flies.

Meuh!

Even a bovine can arouse a Mesopotamian god if her hindquarters are shapely (*binûtam kazbat*).

The first representations of the Egyptian goddess of love, Hathor, in the sixth dynasty (circa 2500 BCE) were in the form of a cow: some can be seen in the Egyptian Museum in Cairo. Later depictions show her with a horned headpiece and holding the sun-disk. She was at various times mother, daughter and wife of Ra.

In some versions of the myth of Io, Zeus turned his latest conquest into a heifer in order to hide her from his wife Hera, who then sent Argus Panoptes, the all-seeing giant, to watch over Io and prevent Zeus from visiting her. She must have still been desirable as a heifer, since she later gave birth to Zeus's daughter Keroessa and a son Epaphus. (It ended badly for Argus, who was killed by Hermes although his hundred eyes ended up as the ocellate decorations on peacock feathers.)

The name Eglah, one of the lesser known of the eight wives of King David in the Bible, means 'heifer'.

Gertrude Stein had a thing about the bovine too. She wrote about 'making a cow come out', which meant (it is safe to infer) bringing Alice B. Toklas to orgasm.

A big perhaps

'Mungkin' was a Malay word I became aware of hearing very often (and even used a lot myself) when I worked in Indonesia, essentially because my limited knowledge of the local *lingua franca* required me to listen very carefully indeed to understand anything at all. 'Mungkin' expressed a certain hesitancy and reluctance on the part of native Indonesians to commit themselves, and perhaps it wasn't surprising I was hearing it since I was trying to get them to commit themselves to work for our health project. That was why I had adopted it myself: I had to keep my options open when I didn't fully understand what conclusions they might beget.

Now I read of an anthropologist who spent a year doing fieldwork (Stephen Pax Leonard) in the town of Qaanaaq in north-western Greenland, one of the most northerly permanent settlements in the world; he writes that 'ammaqa' ('perhaps') was among the common Inuit words that floated through his conversations with the locals. Going into the dark winters, this expression of disengagement more than the solitude or lack of light led him into a kind of depression. To go beyond the borders of his ontological safety zone and find the local people unbudgingly non-committal must have been exasperating. 'Perhaps' is surely a word that expresses all the ambivalence of indigenous peoples about the benefits of modernity. And not just indigenous ones. Jacques Derrida was surely on safe ground when he asserted that 'no category for the future is more appropriate than that of the "perhaps"'.

It has been written that Flaubert discovered the pivotal importance of 'peut-être' the further he worked his way into *Madame Bovary*. The forthright statements of the traditionally omniscient narrator give way to hedgings and equivocations: 'Should she write to her father?' Emma wonders. 'It was too late, and perhaps she regretted not having given herself to the man.' Flaubert's work marks the hinge at which literature lost its wholeness and totality (as mourned by Balzac) and became 'decadent' – fragmentary and haunted by contingency. That is what the adverb 'perhaps' signals. The omniscient narrator of realistic fiction was no longer a feasible notion – hence the indirect free style of his scandalous novel *Madame Bovary* – and the narrator, in the future, would be just as hesitant as his subjects. (And as the life of Flaubert inadvertently shows, the novelist of the future would have to be every bit as much social scientist as storyteller.)

'Perhaps' was also Samuel Beckett's favourite word, although his biography suggests there might be something disingenuous about his plays for a depleted world, or at least a gulf between the writer Beckett and the citizen Beckett: a man who really believed in the ultimate futility of all effort wouldn't take arms against Fascist absolutism, as he so courageously did during the Second World War. If the world is indeterminate, then there is still hope.

This kind of scepticism and awareness of contingency has crept into theology too: some contemporary theologians consider that God's existence is also haunted by 'perhaps'; not indicating hesitancy and doubt so much as an openness to risk and the unforeseeable. But as a friend of mine who once studied for the ministry told me, 'ich habe einige meiner Kommentare gelesen und dann alle diese 'vielleicht' gesehen und wußte sofort, daß ich niemals Theolog sein würde' (I read some of my commentaries [on the Scriptures] and then saw all those perhapses and knew, then and there, that I'd never be a theologian). He had become a philosopher, and I reminded him that Nietzsche, in *Beyond Good and Evil*, had foreseen 'the advent of a new species of philosophers... – philosophers of the dangerous 'maybe' in every sense.' These were philosophers who were prepared to move beyond antitheses (which device Nietzsche thought was specious) and their dialectically improved products.

And of course there is the accommodating punk theology of François Rabelais, whose attributed last words were 'Je m'en vais chercher un grand Peut-Être' ['I'm off in search of a big Perhaps.']

Brute events

'A cry doesn't call – it exults.' So writes Gaston Bachelard in his strange little essay on Lautréamont's *Maldoror*. This is perhaps the same ecstatic scream embraced by Antonin Artaud, defiantly affirming itself in a kind of self-immolation. An expression that can't contain itself, according to Socrates in *Philebus*, where he associated the cacophony of opinions with the sounds of people hollering in the street.

Not the kind of extended totemic exultation Vincent van Gogh heard when he painted, though, or the lucid cruelties Antonin Artaud aspired to produce in the theatre – 'outside thought'. Max Ernst wrote of his 1930s' collages, especially 'Loplop the Bird Superior': 'My works from that time were not destined to seduce but to produce howls.'

Underneath your nose

Subodorer: to have a presentiment. To sense a distant event or presence from the faintest premonition or spoor of evidence, as suggested by Littré's definition. From Latin *subodorari*, literally to smell below (the level of consciousness). A shift into the regions of what Wordsworth called 'under-sense'.

Perception is a fish

The Mayan glyph 'catching a fish with the bare hands', which has the syllabic value *tzak*, denotes the act of conjuring. In Scotland, the related activity of trout tickling is called 'guddling' or 'ginniling'.

Metaphorically extended, the glyph also means 'perceiving', 'grasping the occasion' or even 'invoking the spirits'. Its stylised logographic depiction conveys the sense of something evanescent, difficult of access or readily slipping from the grasp. The salmon of knowledge, it might be, briefly caressing the palm of a hand. Scots dialect has a term 'keethin' sicht', used in one of his mystical lyrics by Hugh MacDiarmid, to describe the ability to sense the presence of a salmon by the overlying ripples in the water.

The novelist Iain Banks recalled in an interview that he had once wanted to invent a Scottish version of Google called Guddle.

A lack of knowledge

Those great appeals for childish spontaneity, simplicity, unselfconsciousness and even pure ignorance, as we find them in the poems, philosophy and novels of Blake, Rousseau and Lawrence, show that their authors were singularly ignorant themselves, either as parents or diagnosticians, of the real nature of children and their impulsive, deep craving for order – allied to their thoughtless dispensing of cruelty. Innocence is a very dangerous word to use as a synonym for 'inexperience.'

Contemporary childhood has been idealised in a not always healthy manner. Middle-class children are now reined in and sedated with technology. Adults have become squeamishly intolerant of childish bullying and violence. Such behaviour used to be accepted because that was how children learned to stand up for themselves and deal with bruises – and bruised feelings. And now we have a generation of students who are so 'fragile' they cannot be exposed to upsetting topics at university.

St Augustine wrote that the innocence of children lay in the weakness of their limbs, not their intentions – but the phenomenon of boy soldiers might have checked him.

An honest thought

In an interview with the elderly Leszek Kołakowski, Danny Postel quoted his own lines back to him: 'The opening line of *Metaphysical Horror* reads: "A modern philosopher who has never once suspected himself of being a charlatan must be such a shallow mind that his work is probably not worth reading".' 'Have you ever suspected yourself of being a charlatan?' Kołakowski: 'Certainly. Many times.' Which I take to mean that Kołakowski was dignified enough as a philosopher to despise himself for using tricks of reasoning to get the better of sceptics and opponents.

He was perhaps unknowingly echoing Robert Burton, who said: 'I count no man a Philosopher who hath not, be it before the court of his Conscience or at the assizes of his Intellect, accused himself of a scurrilous Invention, and stood condemned by his own Judgement a brazen Charlatan.' Burton had seen that there were people after the Puritan Revolution who thought sincerity a matter of intensity, of *really meaning it*, and went in willed ignorance of the kind of masked stand-ins variously recruited to do service as persons philosophical: the fool, the cynic, the sceptic, the courtier, the libertine... even the melancholic. Socially deceitful persons, in short. By contrast, openly suspecting yourself of being a charlatan was a way of proofing yourself against it.

Kołakowski was obviously a *genuine* charlatan, which is also the fine distinction made by Isaiah Berlin to describe George Steiner after having been accused of suggesting that he was an ordinary kind of charlatan.

In France, the many who make a profession out of offering insights based on the uniquely penetrating power of their intelligence should really be known as charlacans – *bien évidemment*.

The One

A fine anecdote about receptivity is told by Porphyry regarding his master Plotinus who, deciding to study philosophy at the age of twenty-seven, made his way to Alexandria. He was dissatisfied with every teacher he came across until he heard Ammonius Saccas lecture. 'This is the man I was looking for,' he told his companion, and embarked upon an intensive course of instruction under his new mentor that would last over a decade and inspire him to join the army of Gordian III in its march eastwards: Plotinus wanted to know more about Persian and Indian philosophy. Six hundred years later the Sunni Abassid philosophers would return the compliment by absorbing his doctrines into their speculations on the nature of the godhead.

In utrumque partes

Simon Hoggart's 'law of the ridiculous reverse' states that if the obverse of a statement is self-evidently absurd then the affirmative version wasn't worth making in the first place. This ploy was well known to classical rhetoricians: they would have said that such a statement lacked a *dirimens copulatio* – the balancing or opposing fact to prevent the assertion from being lopsided.

In our PR era the law of the ridiculous reverse can be found almost anywhere you look or listen. Example: imagine a hospital or a university department coming out with its mission statement – 'We are committed to the lowest standards' or 'Our private hospital aims for disappointing rates of patient satisfaction'...

And there's a related phenomenon in titles such as 'The Institute for Human Values in Medicine', where the word *human* gives pause for thought: isn't that a tiny bit reminiscent of *democratic* as in the former German Democratic Republic, or *scientific* as in 'scientific Marxism'?

Smiling on by

Boccaccio writes that the ordinary citizens of Verona gossiped about Dante. 'You see that man?' one of them said to her friend. 'He goes down to hell when he wants, and comes back with news of those who're down there.' And another would say: 'It must be true: so that's why his beard is frizzy and his skin tanned.' And Alighieri would walk past them with a little smile on his face – 'sorridendo alquanto'.

Surveillance techniques

The presiding presence of the contemporary world must be the mischievous cambion Asmodeus, who lifted the roofs off houses in all the districts of Madrid in Luis Velez de Guevara's fantastic novel *El Diablo cojuelo* (1641) so that its rascal student hero – as a reward for loosing the devil – could capture humans in the secret recesses of their private lives. When the blind John Milton introduced the 'Aerie Microscope', that new-fangled optical device, into *Paradise Regained* thirty years later, he seemed to think its principal function was to peer into houses. Satan in his poem speaks of the device that allows him to see 'Outside and inside both, pillars and roofs / Carv'd work, the hand of famed Artificers, / In Cedar, Marble, Ivory or Gold.'

Both writers were probably familiar with the second-century satirist Lucian's dialogue 'Icaro-Menippus: An Aerial Expedition', in which the character of that name recounts a journey to the moon and Jupiter on wings 'borrowed' from an eagle and a vulture. On the moon, he initially has difficulty seeing the Earth; then he spots the Colossus of Rhodes and the tower of Pharos (two of the seven wonders of the ancient world) and in no time he can see 'everything as clear as possible: looking down to Earth, I beheld distinctly cities and men, and everything that passed amongst them; not only what they did openly, but whatever was going on at home, and in their own houses, where they thought to conceal it.'

When his interlocutor asks him how it was possible for him to see into houses, Menippus replies that the philosopher Empedocles (who just happened to be living on the moon) told him to take off his vulture's wings and wear only eagle's wings: this gave him a vision of the private sphere that was both sharp and cold. Being above (and privy) to the private life of others it seems only natural that a social critique should follow.

Asmodeus isn't just the patron saint of paparazzi and journalists, and Menippus their literary model; they are the forebears of the secret services worldwide. The remit of the professional detective seems to have originated with this legend, which became even better known in the eighteenth century through Alain-René Lesage's French adaptation: 'detect' derives from the past participle of the Latin *detegere*, which means to expose or disclose, or more literally 'to unroof'.

Not on his lips

In *How to Kill a Dragon*, the linguist Calvert Watkins notes, citing scholarly sources, that some words in the lexicon have always been avoided by classical poets as 'unpoetic'. He gives as an example the Greek term *emporos* or 'merchant', reference to which is not found once in Homer's work although mercantile cities and routes – and not just Phoenician ones – are known to have flourished in the eastern Mediterranean from the early Bronze age onwards.

Adam Smith (a thinker of surprising depth and insight) suggests why, in his *Lectures on Jurisprudence*: 'These are the disadvantages of a commercial spirit. The minds of men are contracted and rendered incapable of elevation, education is despised or at least neglected, and heroic spirit is almost utterly extinguished.' That was while he was laying the statutes in his Glasgow lectures for a future where 'every man... becomes in some measure a merchant.'

Social confidence

'Avoir l'air emprunté' goes the French expression: to appear awkward, embarrassed or ill-at-ease means to have a borrowed look: it applies to the person rather than the clothes. I often have this look. Madame de Sévigné speaks of a character about whom nothing is false or simulated ('Rien n'est faux ni emprunté chez elle'), and Saint-Simon, by way of contrast, has the Duchess of Chartres feeling 'empruntée' (clumsy and gauche) on a visit to St Cloud as if it 'were an unknown land'. In other words, the authentic person will be original, graceful and witty, knowing just what to do in any given situation, and never giving the impression of having taken her lines from anyone else (not even from Littré).

This presence of mind surely has something in common with the 'panache' recommended by Edmond Rostand in his play *Cyrano de Bergerac* – a popular success from its Paris premiere in 1897 onwards and one of Gérard Depardieu's best film roles – as a philosophy for life: 'the kind of courage which, at ease in situations, frames and defines them with wit. If renunciation or sacrifice is involved, a consolation of attitude is what one adopts.'

Tongue-tied

Paul Valéry met Joseph Conrad in London in 1922 and had tea with him in Canterbury the following year: he wrote that Conrad had a fine Occitan twang (he had embarked on his first coaster under a captain who came from Valéry's natal town of Sète) but a horribly thick accent when he spoke in his adopted English. This amused him no end. 'To be a great writer in a language which one speaks so badly is a rare and eminently original thing', he wrote in *Sujet d'une conversation avec Conrad*. Valéry would not have known that Conrad had first learned his English in the port of Lowestoft.

A related moment occurred when in September 1884 Nietzsche paid a courtesy visit to the Swiss writer Gottfried Keller, whom he greatly admired, and was appalled by the great man's 'terrible German' and the laborious way he expressed himself in conversation. The pianist Robert Freund, who reported this meeting (*Memoiren eines Pianisten*), says that Keller for his part confided to him at their next encounter that he thought the visiting ex-professor from Basle completely batty – 'ich glaube, dä Kerl ischt verruckt'.

Fabergé design

The most accurate observation about the young Nabokov? 'He can write, but he's got nothing to say.' The writer who was about to become 'the master of the genre of silence' judges the young harlequin whose precision was of a different kind. Isaac Babel made the above remark to Ilya Ehrenburg.

Certainly, Nabokov made sure later in life that he was never caught in public without being dressed up as V. V. Nabokov, author. He was a good chess player, but too fastidiously controlling to risk defeat by playing living opponents (so he worked self-vyingly on chess problems). He disliked television, but was persuaded to appear for a 'live' interview, on Bernard Pivot's television show *Apostrophes* (May 30, 1975): Pivot plied him with questions, and Nabokov read prepared answers, in French, from his famous 3 x 5 inch index cards while attempting to hide them behind a pile of his books in French translation. He spoke for an hour while Pivot, now and again, offered him some more 'tea', and our author looked very pleased at being able to give Pivot all the right answers to his questions. This is what the French would readily have recognised as an 'oralisation de l'écrit'. It suggested to me that Babel saw something in the young Nabokov that I hadn't spotted until then: he is a *taxidermist*.

Nabokov would surely have known that his contemporary Charles Van Doren had to resign from his post as a teacher of English at Columbia when it emerged that his apparently spontaneous replies to questions on a TV quiz show in 1957 had been prepared in advance.

Fremd

My six-year-old daughter, on hearing me make a gender slip in German – corrected by her mother as we talked at table – piped up in my defence with the following pledge: 'Er kann nichts dafür, er kommt nicht aus unsrem Land' [He can't help it, he doesn't come from our country]. She had established my credentials as her alien father, who was accordingly to be cherished.

A projected body

I used to think, as a young anatomist, that the larynx – that triangular assemblage of cartilages under exquisite muscle control commonly referred to as the *voice box* – ought to be regarded as the body's revenge on the mind.

Asked about what he remembered of his attendance at Lacan's famously shamanic seminaries, Philippe Sollers said 'it would have been wonderful to have had a video recording of the seminary in order to experience the body emerging from the voice and not the other way around.' (This could be described as a modern take on the ancient Platonic doctrine that 'the soul is older than the body', its attributes being prior to any notions of weight and solidity, whereas the modern assumption is that the mind is an epiphenomenon coming 'after' the physical procession.)

The master's utterance could only take shape inside the resonant hollow bodies of the audience once it had slithered into their ears, this being the organ that relays the intimate to the public. But his would have been no real body, just the phantom one of structuralism.

Love wind kiss

The commingling of human life and divine breath goes back to the dawn of civilisation in Mesopotamia. 'Then the Lord God formed man of the dust of the earth, and blew into his nostrils the breath of life; and man became a living soul.' This was the primordial inspiration; and the breath which gives life is thereafter bindingly associated with the word which gives life: the mouth is the font and egress of the spirit. It is also the case that in early cultures – in which intimate and implicating modern forms of tongue-kissing seem to be unknown, or at least are not commented upon – there is a direct affinity between breathing and kissing. In his book *The Mystic Rose: A Study of Primitive Marriage*, the anthropologist Ernest Crawley writes: 'The typical primitive kiss is contact of the nose and cheek; the Khoyoungtha, for instance, apply mouth and nose to the cheek, and then inhale.'

Remarkably, the seventh article of the papal bull *Ad nostrum,* which was drawn up at the Council of Vienne in 1312 in order to counter the growing heresy of the 'free spirit' adopted by lay Christians in the German-speaking lands (Beghards and Beguines), asserts that while sexual intercourse is not a sin insofar as men and women are prompted to it by natural impulses 'especially in time of temptation', kissing *is* because nature has not inclined us to it. In that troubled century, the Brethren of the Free Spirit – who believed themselves to be perfect (and therefore impeccable) were alleged, besides dispensing with the ministrations of the Church, to indulge in osculation. For the Church, this was proof of their moral turpitude.

As Juliet tells Romeo in Shakespeare's tragedy, 'Then have my lips the sin that they have took.' To which he responds, 'Sin from thy lips? O trespass sweetly urged! Give me my sin again.'

Two Poems

ROBERT MINHINNICK

A Drone above Port Talbot

51°35'07.0"N 28.6'46°3"W
51.585289, -3.774610

For Sally Jones

I dream of the Ffrwdwyllt,
the problems it gives to strangers,
lacking as it does a solitary English vowel.

That river runs backwards for some,
its water in knots and gnarls against the grain
of what they think they understand.
Yes, Ffrwdwyllt...

And because children live beyond words
I ask what are we but such children
laughing at a language in its agony?

I recall boys around a nest,
scattering the younkers. Yellow bills, naked throats.
I still watch that nest disintegrating.

Once at the Plaza we queued to see Anthony Hopkins,
feeling the plush of the red carpet, the crushed corn...
Not even a city, P' Talbot then or now,
but somehow it grew out of a breezeblock church,
a tin-roofed pub... sinter's glass-sharp dew upon its
     dunes.

And Peg Entwistle, what were you
but a pebble skimmed across the Afan?
Yet I imagine you sponging the pantry stone
then swilling the scullery in Broad Street
where an Amazon Prime electric van
is now triple parked against a DPD electric van
double parked beside an Unlimited Sahara...

Dream on, dream on,
my mind continuing down Eagle Street

all the way from Domino's to Mandie's Breakfast Bar
then up to Wetherspoons' the Lord Caradoc –
     first mishtir of Afan
– then the mosque and the Islamic centre...

But the Ffrwdwyllt is forever a dockland river now,
weary of weirs, this sluice, this sewer,
ten thousand Styrofoam stars and Costa cups
and Covid masks crusted together in a floe of scum,
its current feeding the industrial wells of the Works...

If the future is delirious,
Margam for me will always be steel,
then Swansea Bay and the Meridian tower
now filling with sand, its refugees without masks,
redundant as Gower's iron lighthouse...

Once I stood in its restaurant
and looked east at this world,
the stone age, the iron age, together
under the car park of the Twelve Knights hotel,
Capel Mair, the language's sulphuric haze,
forts and ruins, ruins and forts,
neon ribbons of the motorway...
a drowned child washed ashore on an acid wave,
and a sky without chemtrails.

And so, farewell to all,
but last here's 3, Crown Street
with its poet still shuffling her library cards...
Yes, she too will ask what are we but children
laughing at a language in our agony...?
Because children have learned to live beyond words...

---

* 'mishtir' – 'mister', boss.

Menhenet

Joseph Menhenet,
labourer on the railway,
from the Quarry Street tenement in Plymouth
but born in Tavistock.

The rail reached Horrabridge in the late 1850s.
Cornwall was opening up,
its tin and copper meaning California to some...
and I can almost see the callouses
and dirt under Joseph's fingernails.
Half moons, my mother calls their strange eclipse....

Look, I owe these people
nothing, I owe these people
everything. The labourers,
masons, miners, nightwatchmen, hewers, hawkers
publicans, the imbeciles, the highwayman
and every unnamed child scraped out of the blanket,
the ghosts, the geniuses,
some with names in gold
on a school's honours board,
and a scholarship to Jesus.

Yet it is what's not written that interests me,
the tenement rats, forgotten or unrecorded
despite their marks on the census,
prison house and poor house as far as Mozart House,
and then beyond...
Assault and larceny their convictions
but no record of their kindnesses.

Now, I feel my mother wake
as she floats in her electric bed
in the January dark,
frostbitten, stark,
and in this moment I ask who does she think she is
and which name will she decide to use,
the apparitions, stern daughters at her bedside
imploring her to choose...

And I think of Joseph,
The first I can find to blame,
arranging his crumbs of cheese
upon a broken loaf,
examining the dirt whorled in his palms
and all the bloody cuticles
while mumbling a rhyme in a language
he had never seen written down,
and vanishing like the icicles
of his own name.

Three Poems

BETSY ROSENBERG

The Lay of the Host

I spent the plague years in Kiev,
inexplicably smitten with Prince Igor,
no sleep, no rest, you must have heard,
slava, he sang,
darkly, brightly bari,
glory to the people,
furs and wax
amber and honey.
Tomorrow the full moon will rise
on the verge of war
infusing the snow
with the stench of
frozen vainglory
petrol and gore
and thereafter, spring,
the despot's swansong
in a Polovtsian poppy field
and plague no more!

Edvard

Edvard is irresistible,
ah, 'Wedding Day at Ttroldhaugen'
for his silver anniversary
(reminds me of the
"March of the Siamese Children"
from the *King and I* –
watching the action from the
pit as I played,
all mirth and innocence)
And know this: Edvard Grieg
turned down a prestigious
gig in Paris to protest
the injustice of the Dreyfus Affair,
and he accompanies me now along a zig-zag trail
in the gray and yellow twilight
that moistens the warm soil and lavender
down to the Forest of the Moon
where my dog lies buried under a rock
behind the eucalyptus tree
and I think to myself
Everything here is temporary –
but I am still Neanderthal
all mirth and innocence
outside the cave
this century

Remains to Be Seen

I'm talking to myself –
do you hear me?
I said,
Why worry?
I too will go where the future is past
like my kinsman, the little boy from Ubeidiya,
a million and a half years old,
buried with the bones of giant buffalo
and hippos
jaguars and giraffes
we followed out of Africa
to the rift
near Galilee
Okay
so now
what'll I have for lunch?
Green beans with pickled lemons,
and olive oil from Ubeidiya
and I'll stop talking to myself,
you hear me?

The Unending Meditation on Language

Alvin Feinman's Poems as Self-Consuming Artifacts

JAMES GEARY

'I have an instinct for seeking out unsparingly, with tireless, remorseless, religious labor, the highest diving board, and that above the shallowest pools.'

This line, by the American poet Alvin Feinman, who died in 2008, comes from a black notebook, found in the spring of 2017 in an old leather briefcase, among a cache of Alvin's papers I discovered after traveling to the home he and his wife, Deborah Dorfman, had shared for decades in Bennington, Vermont. After Deborah's death in 2015, the property was to be sold, and I went there to retrieve Alvin's manuscripts and books.

Scrawled in pencil in the top-left corner of the notebook's first page is '1952 – or 3', which dates the thoughts on poetry and poetics the notebook contains to the same period in the 1950s during which Alvin composed almost all of his poems, which Dorfman and I collected in *Corrupted into Song*, published in 2016. Along with the black notebook, there were several other notebooks with Alvin's reflections on poetry, later versions of some of the poems published in *Corrupted into Song*, and several dozen poems unknown to me when Deborah and I were preparing the work in that volume.

Alvin's metaphor of the diving board and the shallowest pools serves as both a description of his working method and a fitting epitaph for the verse of this most difficult and taciturn of poets.

In *PN Review 245* (Jan.–Feb. 2019, pp. 32–38), Chris Miller described Alvin's poems as 'at once an allegory/analysis of poetic creation... and an iconic work of aporia or despair'. The notebook entries support this characterization while also clarifying how Alvin himself seems to have regarded his work. 'I was born with a sense, a foresense of failure,' he writes elsewhere in the black notebook. 'I know that nothing I might attain would equal the destiny I should demand. It was from the beginning only a question of disinteresting myself in whatever destiny I came to learn the name of.'

Alvin continues this strain of elegiac, Ecclesiastes-like lament in another entry:

Surely it is an unspeakable sorrow to walk in the jungle of the works of man. Surely it is a weight no living man can bear.
There is one book only that is worth the making.
There is one book only that is not one more evil.
The last book.

The grave, almost grieving tone of the notebooks gives some sense of the remorseless, religious labor Alvin brought to his poems, and the tension between the ambitions he had for his poetry and his seeming certainty that he would fail to achieve those ambitions.

Yet in failing to write the 'last book', Alvin succeeded in writing something more rare, more difficult and, ultimately, far more rewarding: poems that are so inextricably entwined with their own making that they cannot be reduced, resolved or paraphrased into anything other than themselves.

Each Feinman poem is what Stanley E. Fish described as a 'self-consuming artifact': a work that signifies 'most successfully when it fails, when it points *away* from itself to something that its forms cannot capture'. (Fish, Stanley E. *Self-Consuming Artifacts: The Experience of Seventeenth-Century Literature*. Berkeley, CA: University of California Press, 1972, p. 4.) Though Fish was writing about seventeenth-century metaphysical poetry, his theory of self-consuming artifacts offers an entry point into Alvin's poetry, which so forcefully and so successfully resists explication.

Fish outlined two ways of looking at the world: the discursive, rational view in which the world is divided into discrete entities and the anti-discursive, anti-rational view in which those divisions fade. Poetry merges these opposing ways of experiencing and understanding the world, so that the object and our consciousness of the object – the poem and the 'subject' of the poem – become indistinguishable. A poem, Fish writes, is 'a dialectical presentation [that] succeeds at its own expense; for by conveying those who experience it to a point where they are beyond the aid that discursive or rational forms can offer, it becomes the vehicle of its own abandonment'. (Fish, p. 3.)

Alvin's poems constantly enact this dialectical ebb and flow of union, as in 'From a frosted train window', one of the poems discovered along with the notebooks, in which the act of writing – 'an error of desire objectified' – is undermined even as it is articulated, and the poem itself shines 'the clear, / the difficult / ungathered light' by which we see what we can't quite say:

Unwielded locus of all things,
all such and such
here blunted out: tree,
hill, house, overpass
hardly transgress their names.
The literal abstraction here accomplished
knows itself an error of desire objectified,
and you long for the clear,
the difficult
ungathered light.

Writing of Augustine's *On Christian Doctrine*, Fish outlined a method of understanding self-consuming artifacts that applies to Alvin's poetry: 'Augustine, in effect, has made language defeat itself by making it point away from the temporal-spatial vision it naturally reflects. Of language such as this one cannot ask the question, "What does it mean?" for in everyday terms it doesn't mean anything (as a statement it is self-consuming); in fact, in its refusal to "mean" in those terms lies its value. A more fruitful question would be, 'What does it do?'" (Fish, p. 42.)

What Alvin's language does is perform a feat of reverse prestidigitation, making conventional modes of seeing, meaning and knowing disappear before our very minds, directly implicating and involving the reader in an always unconsummated movement towards closure.

In another notebook, one that had the word 'Record' printed on the front, Alvin formulated his own version of the self-consuming artifact theory, as part of a consideration of Donald Davie's *Articulate Energy: An Enquiry into the Syntax of English Poetry*, published in 1955:

key is: consciousness distinguishes <u>and</u> connects in the same awareness[.] to express this inside a one-one oriented demonstrative language, it must become dialectical – i.e. affirm <u>and then</u> deny ... poetry – having more resources than logic-shriveled discursive grammar – can present (to intuition) the total awareness[.]

The total awareness that poetry presents must include the opposing and finally irreconcilable forces that are consciousness – the imperative to distinguish and connect, to affirm and deny, what Alvin describes as 'a doing and undoing' in another newly discovered poem, 'Begin, Prevail':

Begin

              its dawn
As a day begins, not as
An echo shadows through an act, or
After-image blurs the sequent view,
Or grasp prefigured in the poisoning hand

As weather stills, or quickens
In a leaf, as though leaf's leisure
Pleased to speak a wind, or what wind will
Itself awaited, apart

As animals from looking, or a horse
From looking sideward presently
Or slowly bends, head lowering to grass,
Has bent a hill, a distance, outward, far.

Prevail

Stay to these soundings of your sense,
The burning sentence you would wrest
Once turns like bruised hands moving
Through their pain, pain's plaything being;

Stay to the silence you attest, your
Striving's stutter and its swell, its score
Record as the sea records only
Arhythm not a sense, not rhythm

But a beat, a holding rumor, a remorse

Or vow, a doing and undoing that can surge
Into itself, up-furl, or elsewhere
Shatter, hurl, and roll to calm.

Like his poetry, Alvin resisted explanation. Apart from the notebooks, his most extensive recorded remarks come from a November 1999 letter in response to Robert Dorsett, a student of Harold Bloom's at Yale who was writing a paper on Alvin's work. Dorsett asked if there was anything Alvin cared to say about his approach to poetry or his stance toward language. This is part of his reply:

I have always resisted talking about my poems; not only as to explication, but about the 'unspoken' – which the poem so-to-speak interrupts (crystalizes) – which includes the unending meditation on language. Most exactly the poem itself is the site of self-understanding, articulation, of its poetics ... all aspects of its provenance and project, the constraints that govern its formal (and spiritual) economy ... Certainly I subscribe to the idea (Romantic, no doubt) that the poem is the act of discovering more than is known at the outset; that, fatefully, it transforms and reconstitutes language and self and world; that as much as possible would be put in play – and as it were 'used up' – in the paradigmatic poem – (<u>kenosis</u>, theologically).

Alvin here restates the spare, rigorous poetics first set out in his notebooks more than forty years earlier. The poem alone is its own form and substance, its own language and lexicon. There is, in fact, nothing outside the poem itself to refer to or talk about. Such was the impossibly demanding ambition of Alvin's poetry, and the impossibly demanding standard from which he never wavered.

His stance became a source of contention between Alvin and Bloom, friends since their graduate days at Yale. Bloom was an early and fervent supporter of Alvin's work, and he was instrumental in persuading Oxford University Press to publish Alvin's first book, *Preambles and Other Poems*, in 1964. But he was also frustrated by what he felt was Alvin's obstructionism during the publication process – and the seemingly deliberate wasting of his poetic gift.

In late 1963, Bloom wrote a letter to Alvin 'ten minutes after' the two had quarreled about Alvin's attitude toward Oxford University Press's ideas about the *Preambles* dust jacket. Alvin, who had been withholding the full manuscript to continue revising the poems, apparently objected to the dust jacket; Bloom argued that the dust jacket was a commercial decision best left to the publisher, urging him to focus instead on what was inside the book and on the creation of new work. In the letter, posted with 'Destroy this note' written on the envelope, Bloom wrote:

You know that I love you. I also <u>know</u> you to be a very great poet if you will allow yourself to be one. You <u>could</u> write a <u>Circumferences</u> [the final poem in *Preambles*] that would be a better poem than <u>Notes</u> or <u>The Rock</u>. But only by <u>writing</u>, by releasing exuberance <u>into words</u>, rather than in this endless interior monologue you conduct. Put that ceaseless meditation into a daily journal; make a rule for yourself henceforward, to <u>write</u> after you <u>read</u>. What I fear for you is waste, loss, dispersal; you have already squandered a decade of early maturity, with only one volume of lyrics to show for it, and only 8–12 of those really remarkable. Turn your discipline on yourself; you have had time to <u>work</u>, and yet you haven't <u>worked</u>. If it seemed too solitary to induce externalization of your broodings, that is over now; you have a publisher, you will have an audience. I'm not asking you to debase yourself to attract that audience; but don't insanely impede every sensible attempt to get that audience that others will make for you.

Alvin did not follow Bloom's advice. He neither kept a journal after the notebooks he wrote in the early 1950s, nor did he continue to produce a body of new work. He did not insanely impede attempts to acquire an audience, but he did nothing to foster one either.

What he did do was tirelessly, remorselessly, religiously compress an unending meditation on language into dense, dazzling poems that instigate a process of self-understanding and discovery that is renewed and left newly unfinished with each reading. As we climb up after him to that highest diving board above the shallowest pool, Alvin kicks away the ladder just as we reach the top.

Two Poems

DEAN BROWNE

Other

Spring proliferates blown red roses!
I mean behind the sunlit glass.

Thrushes ruckus the fresh green hedges!
I mean I'm trying to sleep here.

Red squirrel and coot hurrah the park!
I mean the swings are empty.

Nothing's far from fading.
A warped fence for your troubles.

Yet the salmon was never fresh here.
I mean my heart was torn.

I mean my future was sonnet-shaped
and you walked at the volta.

I lay you down now like a kitchen knife!
I mean sorry, wrong number.

What a moment to play Angel Olsen!
(It could have been Agnes Obel.)

But o the roquefort and beaujolais,
the kimonos some green tomorrow!

And o my clever wine-high lover!
I mean around the corner

like the sea: sooner or later.
Sloshing in with the *Mary Celeste*!

She is growing small bones
inside her, and the consequence

will be ours to love!
I mean I hope for other

than cataloguing my losses
as those one-trick prodigies

pony up, all shadows and facets
under my jeweller's loupe.

The Fates

It's Herr Mann, the neighbour, out walking his *Hund.*
That's him stalled at the lights and what does he do?
Correct. He steps into traffic. May chance guide Herr
    Mann.
And what does he see next, what does the dog?

That's right. A greengrocer hawking spiny pineapples.
Seedsellers. A barista emptying ashtrays on a café
    terrace.
Shining counterfeit watches. And who can tell me?
Top marks. The palm-reader set up one end of the
    pingpong table.

I saw you walk towards me from a long way off, she goes.

And you guessed, she grips his palm. Herr Hund rests
    on his paws.
Chilly as the ass of a cherub posted over a grave,
she says. But Herr Mann's hearing has never been
    acute.

Do you imagine Herr Mann stood to hear his palm
    speak
or that the terrier tugged him back into traffic, away
from the heavy-ringed fingers? Mull it over, but not too
    long.
The pingpong players are turning their paddles hand to
    hand.

Three Poems

WILLIAM WOOTTEN

Globe & Chart

In the Heroic Age, departing ships were mourned as they popped down
Beneath the edges of the world before they would, perhaps,
Resurface with hulls crammed full of veterans, slaves and booty.
To the widows, wives, children and old men who perched on harbour rocks
Or those aboard who watched the small coast sink or rise to them,
The planet they encountered was growing slightly spherical.

A sea on a flat planet would be perceived as different:
On clear days the watched sails would dwindle slowly till the point
Where they would vanish, then return to good binoculars.
And yet no telescope could reach beyond that limit where
Magellan and his men flipped keel then dropped towards the stars.
Young children watching from a pier beside a shipping lane
Would map adventurous minds onto a world whose certain margin
No ship could hope to sail beyond and ever journey back.

Wise Women

Why is it the three sisters never marry?
Grey eyed and distant, they visit us sometimes.
Telling us they worry how we are,
For their lives lie perfect as a star
In its own freezing, the high chimes
Of their voices as elementary

As maths. They pity us, perhaps – do they
Pity us? – watching as we age before their glance.
Or is it merely that we puzzle them?
Imagine someone with a flawless gem
Should see a flower-seller and so chance
To wonder if the fresh blooms on display

Might be as wonderful in their few hours
As countless years of changeless jewellery.
Perhaps the wistful smile their lips hold back
Is that, a richness that conceals a lack
Of something else that lives could be,
Heartbreaking and transitory as flowers.

Cellar Door

A friend of C.S. Lewis spelled it 'Selladore'
(Like 'the far land of Spare Oom where eternal summer reigns
Around the bright city of War Drobe'). Yet when they say,
If they still do, that 'cellar-door' is lovelier
In sound than all the other words we have in English,
Their point is usually that what it means is dull,
No more than a cellar door.

                    When I was a child,
We never had a cellar-door, nor did my friends,
But in an August beneath my grandmother's house in Maine,
A house which smelled of wood and fresh-baked cookies,
There was a cellar, full of what the world upstairs
No longer had much call for: family mementoes,
Old skis and bric-a-brac, and shelves of books
Kept from my grandmother's Ohio childhood.
Some names that were brand new in the time when she was young,
Like Thornton W. Burgess or Albert Bigelow Paine,
Had since grown into children's classics in the States,
But most of them were names to baffle Barnes and Noble,
And even the *Oz* books there weren't all by L. Frank Baum.
I remember taking one of them to read upstairs.
Its hero was pulled away from Kansas by his kite
(I was given a cloth kite, blue with a red whale,
Which swam into the sky above the blueberry bushes).
It was odd to think the little girl who read these books
When icehouses were still filled with ice from winter lakes
Now watched TV and read only the newspaper.

She let me keep *The Hollow Tree and Deep Woods Book*.
The rest she kept down there until she died, when my aunt,
Detecting mildew, made a bonfire of them all.
Right now, I cannot see a door with certainty,
But if there was a door there rather than a hatch,
It might have been a whitewashed one or else plain wood,
No more exciting than a wardrobe door would be,
The sort that has two mirrors in (this is not the film),
Reflecting a child in the spare room one day
In summer till the old fur coats were pushed aside
And the sound of crushing mothballs became the crunch of snow.

In *The Farthest Shore*, which is by Ursula K. Le Guin
And which I must have read at roughly the same time
I lost my grandmother, there is a Selidor,
The last island in the West, bleak and full of dragons.
But the dragons, whose language keeps the true names of all things,
Have forgotten how to speak. The meaning and the magic
Are draining from the world. So Ged, or Sparrowhawk,
As the archmage is known, deserts the life above
To walk into the rainless cities of the dead
Seeking wholeness in dark names and absences,
Like a boy making his way down disappearing steps
Into a musty jumble where the light is gone
To search for what to bring back through the cellar-door.

Talking with Gerry Cambridge of *The Dark Horse*

RORY WATERMAN

The Dark Horse is now in its twenty-seventh year, and you've been its sole main editor throughout. How have the challenges you face as an editor changed over the years? Have you always stuck to the same principles?

Various things have changed. In the early days a definite challenge was getting enough quality work, particularly prose, to put into the magazine. That's far less the case now. Issues around representation and gender balance are much more prominent, rightly, now than they were in 1995 when I didn't give much thought, for instance, as to what the balance between men and women in the magazine was. That changed relatively quickly though. I think the primary aim of editing a 'little' magazine is to hold out by one's own lights for the best writing, prose and poetry, that one can find. With that in mind, I probably have stuck broadly to the same principles with which I started. I am, with complications, the same solitary reader I was in my Ayrshire caravan when I founded the journal and wanted to read poems and prose that affected me at a level deeper than the merely academic. I may be a more sophisticated reader now, but that general aim, of wanting to publish work that connects deeply on a human level, remains the same.

'Deeper than the merely academic.' That first word is loaded, isn't it? Do you think that is – or was – too often forgotten or ignored by some editors? Did you conceive of The Dark Horse *as a refuge from the increased academisation of poetry?*

Is 'deeper' 'loaded'? It can be hard to tell these days what you're 'permitted' – if you pay credence to such things – to speak about without rousing opprobrium from some quarter or other. I wouldn't wish to speak about what is forgotten or ignored by fellow editors. Editing properly is a tough job. Each editor, I guess, follows their own aesthetic and hopes it will be matched by a readership. In founding *The Dark Horse* I think, in retrospect, I wanted to produce a magazine I would have found interesting to read had I been 'only' a poet and reader. It's an honour to encounter acute and often brilliant minds via the pages of a journal you're editing. Was it Howard Sergeant who called publishing a little magazine 'self-education in public'? I approve of that notion. In terms of the journal's aesthetic, my own tastes arise out of the peculiarities of my own character, biography and background: largely uneducated, self-taught, quite unliterary until my early twenties, the child of working-class Northern Irish Catholic parents who were part of the Irish diaspora. Philip Hobsbaum, my dear carnaptious friend, once wrote to me after I'd annoyed him with an outrageous opinion the following immortal words: 'Gerry, you are a literary amateur, and the reason you

think there is no such thing as a literary education is because you have not had one.' Exactly. Yet that is the cornerstone of everything I have done with *The Dark Horse*.

Do you remember the 'outrageous opinion'? If so, do you stand by it?

I do remember it, and I don't stand by it. I was newly, and new-bumptiously, installed as poet in residence at Hugh MacDiarmid's cottage in Biggar. I wrote to Philip that, *of course*, most poetry criticism was really only a higher form of copyediting and that I was much more interested in *why* a critic thought something than in *what* they thought. Which, naturally enough, roused him to respond. He later recommended me though as a writer of criticism, mainly monographs on individual poets and their work, to Jay Parini for Scribners in the US which led later to ten essay commissions by Jay for the 2003 *Oxford Encyclopaedia of American Literature*. I wrote around 150,000 words for these two publishers combined, over some six years. I was, literally, paid to be a student. I was very fond of Philip though I understand why some people took against him. I have, as Norman MacCaig would say, relishing recollections of those days. I got to know Philip quite well when he retired from Glasgow, from around 1997 till his death in 2005. I took some of the last good photographs of him, which the broadsheets used to accompany his obituaries.

Hobsbaum founded what I think was Scotland's first postgraduate Creative Writing course at Glasgow at about the same time you founded the magazine. To what extent do you think the two were complementary endeavours? What effect do you think the proliferation of programmes like that has had on contemporary poetry?

Yes, Philip thought creative writing should be at the centre of the academy, partly to help teach students humility about the work they were writing academic essays on. I don't think creative writing departments and little magazines are particularly complementary, except in the obvious way. I don't know what effect the creative writing departments have had on contemporary poetry. It would be easy, out of my natural contrariness, to denounce them, of course, but then I remember a little writing group I used to go to in Irvine, Ayrshire, in the early eighties which I found sustaining, and my early unofficial mentorships/correspondences with George Mackay Brown and the Galloway poet William Neill; these, I guess, were my version of the same. Yet, as long as the work is good, I have always had a liking for outsiders, mavericks, unexpected spirits in poetry, such as the Kintyre poet Angus Martin of Campbeltown, a herring fisherman in his youth and latterly a postman, who has written a small but significant body of valuable and perdurable poems. I can't imagine such figures attending a creative writing department to get a degree; as a poet, I ally and identify myself with them.

You've published in the most recent issues two articles defending poets who have become, in some quarters, untouchable: Rob A. Mackenzie's analysis of charges of Fascism in the work of Toby Martinez de las Rivas, and the Scottish performance poet Jenny Lindsay's own account of her 'cancellation' for alleged transphobia. Though there are Scottish connections in both cases, these aren't poets one might otherwise readily associate with the magazine. What made you want to commission these pieces?

The same instinct that made me criticise William Logan's review of Keith Douglas's *Selected Poems* in, I think, *The New Criterion*, when I was on a panel in the US and Professor Logan was in the audience: a reaction against unfairness and perceived misrepresentation. Both the de las Rivas and Jenny Lindsay instances have parallels: the first involving an accusation of Fascism, the second an accusation of transphobia, and both, to me, easy and grossly untrue slurs fomented by social media and other online activity. Many people took the magazine's response to the former case as a defence of a white, establishment, traduced poet; in reality, it was a forensic analysis, by Rob A. Mackenzie, of slack critical writing put to potentially career-wrecking ends. There was nothing personal whatever about it; I had never met de las Rivas and barely knew his work up to that point. Both these cases are related to the current puritanism in Poetry World, which manifests as intolerance, moral superiority, desire for punishable victims, and attempts at no-platforming and damage to people's livelihoods.

What would you say to those in the arts who have sought to do this damage, or to those who do not want to publish or perform alongside these poets? And what would you say to the suggestion – which I have heard put with some passion – that you have only given voice to one side of these arguments?

I don't have anything to say to those individuals. Obviously, what they decide to do is their own choice. As a general rule though, my response to unfair attempts at no-platforming and attempted disruptions of people's livelihoods is, if I'm in a position to do so, to give those individuals opportunities and, frankly, to go against what a particular consensus, at least in a part of poetry Twitter, may think. Hence I featured de las Rivas in interview in the subsequent issue of *The Dark Horse* to the one in which Rob Mackenzie's critique of Dave Coates's blogpost appeared, and I gave space to Jenny Lindsay to explore and express in a wider cultural context what had happened to her.

As for the 'giving space to only one side of the argument' critics: the world is full of armchair editors. If I'd taken all the unasked-for advice I'd been given over the years I'd never have published the journal. Regarding the de las Rivas affair, the online consensus was that that

poet was fascistic. Apart from *PN Review*, as far as I know, the *Horse* was the only journal that gave voice to the opposing view. So why give space to the 'other side' when it had already been so abundantly aired on social media and online and the poet so effectively traduced and made a pariah? As for the Jenny Lindsay essay, the number of women (and some male) readers who contacted me privately after it was published expressing gratitude at my 'courage' for publishing the article made me realise how rare it was for such an essay to appear in a literary journal. So the *Horse* was, you could say, redressing a sort of balance in that instance. That being the case, why blunt the point that was being made? The journal was responding to something in the wider culture. It would have diluted its effect to aim for some kind of balance within the magazine's pages themselves. Also: the *Horse* is a typical 'little' magazine, by commercial standards, and it only appears twice a year. I have to choose carefully what I'm going to feature within those parameters. We can't do everything. And I do see the role of a little magazine as being, to a degree, a going against consensus. I strongly believe in a culture of various, disparate little magazines each fighting their own corner, as partisanly as they like. I don't much care whether a magazine is left wing, centrist or right wing. What matters is that it is interesting, lively and full of personality, without promulgating extreme views.

What do you make of Jenny Lindsay's story being picked up in The Spectator *by Nick Cohen?*

It sold some copies for us. I was grateful to him for that. To his credit, he encouraged people to buy the journal and not just rely on his account, which had the impossible task of condensing 8,250 words, scrupulously written, on complex issues into a short account for a magazine known for trenchant opinion.

Yes, 8,250 words is a lot! Quite a few years ago now, you gave me one of my first longish magazine commissions – to review a book of William Logan's criticism, as it happens. The Dark Horse *is a bit of a rarity among poetry magazines in that you never publish very short reviews. Why the preference for fewer longer pieces over a greater number of shorter ones?*

Oh, we have sometimes published shorter reviews – but never *very* short. I like to let gifted writers write to the length that covers what they want to say. At the minute we're not running reviews at all as such; our most recent issues have mainly featured longer-form essays on a variety of poetry topics, sometimes contentious ones. Around issue 39, our 'Neglected [Dead] Poets' number, in summer 2018, possibly because I'd been using Twitter more, I began noticing the extreme reactiveness of some elements of the poetry 'community' – so called – and began drawing attention to it, firstly in that issue's editorial. The shift would have been happening before then – Jenny Lindsay in her essay in the issue 42 puts it at around 2015 – but that was when I noticed a change in attitude towards poetry in which the approved politics, morals or viewpoints of poets on various issues was deemed more important than their art. There seemed very little love for the art itself; poetry was used only as an indicator of social mores; the perceived values of a particular poet were considered more significant than how, for instance, they turned a line, used metaphor, or any of those things. One had to be morally pure and good to be a significant artist, an attitude I fundamentally disagree with. (Figures like Larkin and Frost are fascinating because they transcend their own failings and make astonishing poems.) That shift, towards a censorious, punitive poetry culture devoid of gaiety – a word I'm fond of – only seems to have intensified since. To some degree, in the last three issues the magazine has engaged and argued with the roots of those attitudes, and what the future holds in that regard we shall see.

Many of the American poets who have appeared regularly in the magazine are associated to some extent with 'New Formalism': Dana Gioia, Julie Kane, Amit Majmudar, Tim Murphy, and Rhina Espaillat, to name only a few. New Formalism has generally been given fairly short shrift by the academy and by most poetry magazines and critics, especially in the US. Is there any connection for you between these two observations?

I think the connection between some of those figures you mention, such as Majmudar and Murphy, and New Formalism is tenuous at best. The *Horse* was associated loosely with that movement in its earliest days, but rapidly established a healthy scepticism. Temperamentally, I'm not a joiner of movements. As proof of my editorial independence I commissioned John Lucas – that bracing bastion of forthrightness and critical candour – to review the showcase anthology of that movement, *Rebel Angels*, in an early issue. On the other hand I made some great friends and met some excellent poets through their association with New Formalism, often at the annual poetry conference set up by Dana Gioia and Michael Peich at West Chester University in Pennsylvania which I must have attended eight or nine times between 1999 and 2016. The gaiety, wit, general good-naturedness and capacity for alcohol of that conference was a phenomenon. I met there figures like Richard Wilbur, Anthony Hecht, Louis Simpson, X J Kennedy, and Dana himself of course, all of whom I used to read in my caravan in Ayrshire. If you'd told me then, in the isolated days of the mid-eighties in rural Ayrshire, often in howling winters, when I was beginning to write my own poems, that I'd meet some of these figures fifteen years later – the legendary ones like Wilbur and Hecht particularly – I'd have been astonished. Yet it happened.

You published Wilbur in issue 1, I believe. And I know you corresponded with him, and with plenty of others of comparable esteem: Hecht, Seamus Heaney, George Mackay Brown. You once described their letters to you as 'almost talismanic items', and told me you admired the 'quiet authority of these writers'. What did they teach you in those early days, beyond what is in their poems? Are you willing to share any insights and what they mean to you?

My most significant early influences, both for their poetry and how they comported themselves as artists, were George Mackay Brown and Galloway's William Neill. George wrote comments on poems I sent him and returned them, and we had a fairly regular correspondence that lasted from 1985, the summer I first met him, to the year of his death, 1996. I'd often visit him if I was in the islands, which I was frequently in those days. William Neill was a very different personality from George. He could, even in age, be quite cantankerous and was a considerable linguist. He wrote in Gaelic, which he'd learned, Scots, which he was native to, and English. He also knew Latin and Greek. He called himself proudly a 'makar' and 'a maker of formal verses'. From both of them I learned, I guess, a respect for the tradition of the art. But I also absorbed as it were by osmosis attitudes that I'd be hard put to pin down. From George perhaps a relative indifference to London-centric prize culture etc; from Willie, who was a maverick of sorts, the idea that being an outsider was no bad thing. George handwrote his letters in careful, methodical script – the words placed, as he described it somewhere, of an old crofter's speech, like rocks in a drystane dyke. Willie's letters were word-processed, with handwritten emendations. But they were both men who saw, I think, the practice of the art as being something of a way of life without frills or hoo-ha or the idea that they were engaged in anything more hierarchically special, however fascinating to them personally, than a carpenter or a mechanic. George's letters did have a talismanic quality for me. One he wrote to me on Hogmanay 1985 that the postman wrapped with an elastic band round the handle of my caravan door to stop the gale from blowing it away was instrumental in everything that followed after for me in poetry, including the *Horse*. He wrote an introduction to my first book of poems, *The Shell House*. He wrote the reference for the Scottish Arts Council, a year earlier, that helped me get a writing bursary, with some of which I began the magazine. The other poet whose letters had something similar to this talismanic quality was Seamus Heaney, though my correspondence with him was far less regular. I also wish I'd written to Ted Hughes. At the time I thought he would be unlikely to respond to an unknown living in a country caravan in Ayrshire, of my background. Now, of course, I realise that might have piqued his interest.

Which poets do you correspond with now? And where does that 'quiet authority' endure, do you think, if anywhere, among the younger generations?

My longest lasting recent correspondences by traditional post have been with Niall Campbell, Richie McCaffery and Naush Sabah. I don't think of 'quiet authority' residing in the younger generation. I believe that's something you attain with age, if at all.

I know the late North Dakotan poet Tim Murphy sent you a full manuscript, in the early days of the magazine, and invited you to take your pick. I loved Tim, but rarely agreed with him about anything, one example being his knee-jerk opposition to all more experimental verse.

Yes, that story is true about Tim Murphy. Though he glamorised himself as having 'worked on a farm' in his youth I don't believe he had, quite, not in the way I had. But he was a great fan of Burns and I think was tickled by my having been raised in Ayrshire and founding the magazine there. I recognise in him an authentic poet of substance who wrote a small body of memorable poems; a Murphy *Selected* would be a fine thing, though latterly he wrote too much. I published him frequently in the earlier issues of the *Horse*, and wrote an epistle to him in habbie stanza which is in *Madame Fi Fi's Farewell and Other Poems*. When I first encountered him in 1995 he was a millionaire venture capitalist who asked me what was the minimum amount it would take for me to attend the first West Chester Poetry Conference that year. I hadn't a clue about such things and said '$500'. Back came a cheque for that amount. In the interim, I felt uneasy about accepting the money and so returned it with a note explaining that I felt accepting it might compromise my editorial independence. He returned it to me, with a letter encouraging me to accept the money simply as a donation for the magazine. On that basis, I did. When he won the New Formalism sonnet prize a few years later, he donated the $1000 cheque to the *Horse*. By that time of course I had already accepted numerous of his poems so the issue of editorial compromise had been laid to rest. An interesting, colourful man; but unappreciative, as you say, of anything that wasn't metred and rhymed.

Do you think editing The Dark Horse *has had any discernible influence on the poems you've written?*

Only insofar as editing and assessing work for a journal for quarter of a century has perhaps sharpened my ability to do the same with my own writing.

For all my time editing the *Horse*, my own poetry is – for me – the vital centre of it all. It is a fine thing to be involved in a great art at whatever level, the practice of which is an act of self-realisation, a journey into the inner life, and becomes a way of being.

Your new collection, The Light Acknowledgers, *is a real emotional chiaroscuro. In the title poem you describe 'the incandescent pollens / of our days'; elsewhere, a pining for when 'all worldly happiness was centred / on a redpoll's / or a linnet's egg'. How has getting older altered your perspectives?*

I'm now 63. So there's rather more behind me than there is ahead. And, as Edward Thomas wrote, 'The past is a strange land, most strange.' I find musing about what has happened in one's life fascinating. My verse tends to have more retrospection now than when I was younger. I'm aware increasingly of wanting a stripped-back clarity in my verses which carries the weight of experience. What one wants creatively and what one ends up writing, of course, are two different things. It's good to be surprised.

'Buying Groceries on a Windy Day on Papa Westray', in the new book, is the only 'serious' poem I can think of written predominantly in amphibraic hexameter. It works: the poem feels at once free, happily anxious, and perennially perambulatory. But what on earth made you want to do this?

William Neill, the Galloway poet, said the metre was impossible in English. So I thought I'd try and prove him wrong, and wrote the poem as an exercise. That was almost thirty years ago. Then I discovered it among my papers and thought it had potential, simply as the sound was so different from, say, pentameter. So I reworked it for the book. In its favour, the galloping rhythms and the long lines seemed appropriate to a small Atlantic island surrounded only by sea horizons on a windy day. I have no problem waiting many years for a poem to be ready to publish. A couple of other poems in that book are thirty years old; the most recent were written only six months before the book was published. It pleases me that – at least I tell myself this – no one could probably tell which was which.

Are more of your poems the product of unhappiness than of its opposite? Apparent self-reproach is a common thread in your poetry, often wedded to a wry wit. In Notes for Lighting a Fire, *for example, there is the 'gutted' pub where now your 'face fits'.*

I don't know. I think some of them are happy enough – those dealing with physical phenomena like light, and elements of the natural world, which has always fascinated me – both of which connect to my earlier life as a natural history photographer. But perhaps as you get older you can speak with more unaffected gravitas about things less happy. Which is not an unhappy activity. There is something deeply satisfying about making art, by your own lights, which gets to grips with what you perceive as reality – wresting or patterning chaos into form and rhythm.

Four Poems

NICKI HEINEN

Deer in Clissold Park

1

Shapes like spotted play-doh, limbs sticking out in
held agency.

2

Bleary sunset, church spire silhouetted in its frame.
The green of the grass phosphorous bright. The stag
dips his bejewelled head and nips the grass. Eyes
like buttons on a dress shirt.

3

Only the enclosure can stop the running deer from
spilling out into clipped lawns and the gentle canals
of the park, and into grey London beyond. If they
could run out, they would stop on the rain-soaked
tarmac and clip their hooves till the cars dissolved.

4

She looks so fragile it's frightening. White spotted
and lop-tailed, her blush fur shines even when she
is an O in the distance. Up close, she shakes a naked
throat and the fringes of her eyelashes collect pol-
len.

5

Do the sleeping deer become invisible once there is
no-one there? Melting into midnight dew, the trees
spread their aged branches. Night birds call. I want
to go to the park after it is locked, to see if they are
there.

The Sad Dog

The dog sits at the doorway of the exploded barn,
which has no sides and no roof. His tail lies behind
his rump and it lies still. The air is thick with con-
gealed smoke, and occasional sparks light up the
dark night. The dog is alone. The dog is sad. Its eyes
are pennies. Each one shines with tears. Bodies are
lying over the ashy floor.

Convex

The ocean comes back and back
that sound of shucking, of static
like a ball with pins inside rolling
forever. Warm sand stretches
to the right and to the left
my feet wet with sea
my eyes lit with it
my body sure, head damp
the scent of beach
clean and salty
the sky a queen's sash
and the sun, the oldest one
shuddering down in solitude
over me and over me
till I am intoxicated with pale heat
half cut with blue
ill with the beauty of it

Shade

A red light yes, and a red door, with a red doorknob.
A red ceiling, with red cornices, a red floor, a confu-
sion of red cats, and red dogs, masterful red lamp-
shades, and red curtains, with violently red swags.
I sit, in a red dress, with red shoes and red hair,
smoking a red cigarette. The cushions are heavy red.
The sky in the red window is exploding red, and the
rain is red, and the clouds are red. My voice is red.
It screams 'Give me more'.

Four Poems

TOON TELLEGEN

Translated from the Dutch by Judith Wilkinson

Playing Field

If I stood on the banks of the Lethe,
would I drink?

I know exactly what I want to forget,
but do I really want to forget it,
do I want to stop feeling the pain of it?

behind me the immense playing field of my conscience,
where good and evil sleep in each other's arms
and joy and sorrow attack and devour each other
        till they're obliterated

I need to think,
I need to start thinking at last

I don't drink.

Write on Walls

Write on walls:
'Oh Schopenhauer, it's more than the will...'

it's pain and mood-swings
that make life unliveable

arriving in their galleons
with one-legged captains and Jolly Rogers

it's poisonous daisies and frivolous snakes
        in the lush grass of bliss

write your name on walls and let yourself weather.

I Stayed on the Main Road

My brother,
he took sideroads, went looking for danger, got lost,
had adventures,
retraced his steps, but never for long,
looked back, looked sideways, looked up,
was desperately happy,
broke arms, legs,
walked in rain, snow, fog, darkness,
met the most peculiar people

I stayed on the main road,
a willing prey to those who hunt for people
who stay on main roads and miss their brother

at night I hear him cry.

All Numbers Smaller than Two

In me are all numbers smaller than two:
they pursue each other, hound each other, almost overtake
  each other

outside in the twilight the others whirl about,
the two, the three, the ten –
'we're making something of our lives,' they cry, 'you should
  do the same...!'

I hear my one and my zero pant,
I feel the monotonous weariness of their existence –
they are my inner being, my essence, my self

one day they will seize each other,
say something to each other that I can't decipher
and multiply together

the answer will be of an unimaginable simplicity.

Toon Tellegen, *Tot de winter er op volgt*,
Querido, Amsterdam 2021.

Reviews

A Bright Shovel of a Face

Valzhyna Mort, *Music for the Dead and Resurrected*
(Bloomsbury Poetry) £9.99

Reviewed by Rebecca Hurst

Born in Minsk in 1981, and so living out the first decade of her life in the waning Soviet Union, Valzhyna Mort spent her time after school in the family kitchen listening to her grandmother's stories of war and political persecution, a litany of loss and trauma that were not reflected in the poet's school history or literature classes. As Mort described in an interview with NPR's Morning Edition, growing up in Belarus – a place where by the late 1930s 80 percent of the region's writers and artists had been killed by the Soviet regime – 'the stories of my family, of my dead had no place in official historical narratives'. Instead it was left to the 'test-child exposed to the burning reactor' of her grandmother's memory to reckon with and to write this lost narrative; to find a way of handling, composing, and bringing into the world such incendiary material.

Mort's second English-language collection, *Music for the Dead and Resurrected,* was received into a world freshly attuned to the political and personal repression experienced by the contemporary citizens of Belarus. In the wake of August 2020's post-electoral protests, the collection has been read and reviewed largely from a socio-historic perspective. Largely and justifiably, as Mort herself has discussed the poems in *Music for the Dead* (and her previous collection, *Collected Body*) in terms of a response to the lacuna in both official history and culture of the lived experiences of Belarusian peo-

ple. While the world was riveted by news coverage of mass demonstrations and arrests, Mort's poems seemed extraordinarily prescient. Like the visceral work that has emerged over the past fifteen years from the Belarus Free Theatre, Mort's voice comes bellowing up from a dystopian underworld, where the very 'Streets introduce themselves / with the names of national / murders' ('Bus Stops: Ars Poetica'). In the mythologizing opening poem of the collection, 'To Antigone, a Dispatch', the theme of the individual pitted against state power and brutality is clearly stated: 'Pick me for a sister, Antigone', Mort writes, 'In this suspicious land / I have a bright shovel of a face.'

In addition to historical context and current geopolitics, however, there are other noteworthy elements of Mort's poetry: surreal images spill kaleidoscopically across the page, as do musical rhythms, short and fragmented lines, interrupted/unfinished narratives, and an uncanny crowd of characters. 'My motherland rattles its bone-keys. / A bone is the key to my motherland', says the narrator of the driving, remorseless poem 'An Attempt at Genealogy', which is unlocked by the bone key – a classic trope from the North European tradition of magic tales. The same poem's opening and repeated line – 'Where am I from?' – endures beyond war memorials and state archives.

Folktales, told for ritualistic purposes and emerging from the oral tradition, are a means by which humanity has made sense of the incomprehensible. And the polyphony of folktales, as well as the theme of katabasis – or descent to the underworld – is something that Mort inherited not just from her grandmother but from another Belarusian writer, the Nobel Laureate Svetlana Alexievich. Although Alexievich writes documentary non-fiction, her work is remarkable for both polyphonous voices, and also for surreal, fairytale-like collisions between the natural and human world. In Alexievich's collection of interviews, *Chernobyl Prayer*, the 'Monologue on how we can talk with both the living and dead' opens with the lines: 'A wolf came into the yard in the night. I looked out the window and it was standing there, eyes blazing. Like headlamps'. The monologue could have come from the mouth of Mort's loquacious Baba Bronya, who wields against future catastrophe her terrifying, watchful purse 'that held – / through seven wars – / the birth certificates of the dead' ('Bus Stops: Ars Poetica').

The repeated folkloric motifs in *Music for the Dead* – of apples and Eve, dogs and dog-roses, forests and the sea, sun and moon, birds and trees, skulls and bones, and inanimate objects that suddenly, astonishingly, spring to life – cut through the poems like the folk melodies that cut through Dvorak's classical scores. They are apparent in 'To Antigone's' evocation of magic tales that feature the Slavic primordial goddess/witch, Baba Yaga, intercessor at the boundary between this world and the spirit world:

Once we settle your brother,
I'll show you forests
of the unburied dead.

We'll clean the way only two sisters
can learn a house...

Why bicker with husbands about dishes
when we've got
mountains of skulls to shine?

And again in the remarkable 'Singer', which summons the spirit of another famous character from Russian children's literature, The Little Humpbacked Horse, and the bison, which wanders out of 'the woods of Belaveža' (spanning the border between Belarus and Poland, and the site of the accords that formally ended the Soviet Union) and which is variously transformed as: 'a sylvan angel of history, / a bison of melancholia, / a black van.' Not only enabling Mort's lyrical reckoning with traumatic memory, the folkloric motifs also provide the possibility of both unearthing – with that 'bright shovel' – and of restoring the Belarusian experience.

As with much of Russian and Soviet history, as with much of twentieth-century history, as with the history of empire-building and colonisation, the scale of events can feel at odds with our ability to comprehend them against the specificity of individual human lives. In her Poetry Society lecture *FACE – FACE – FACE: A Poet Under the Spell of Loss* (given in March 2021), Mort grapples with research that has led her to a reckoning with the 9,200 'Belarusian villages burnt to the ground during World War II', 'fire-villages' that lack a monument within Belarus itself, but that burn on in the memories of those who survived, and of their descendants. 'You remember the names of all our dead relatives and know the distance between the burned-down villages', Mort writes in the prose poem 'Baba Bronya', 'But you never remember that you have already told me these stories before.' Yet, the compulsion to tell and retell is also the compulsion behind *Music for the Dead*. How else to reckon with those burned villages? How else to reckon with the radioactive winds that swept across Belarus in 1986, during Mort's own childhood, following the explosion of the Chernobyl nuclear reactor? How else to explicate displacement, genocide, environmental catastrophe and generational trauma, except through language where the lyric hopefully asserts itself, takes root, only to be broken, to fail, to reassert itself and fail again in gaps, in fragments, in silences, in surreal transformations and transferences,

as in 'Nocturne for a Moving Train':

Radiation, an etymology of soil

directed into the future, prepared
a thesis on the new origins of old roots,
on secret, disfiguring missions of misspellings,
on the shocking betrayal of apples,
on the uncompromised loyalty of caesium.

As the Soviet folklorist Vladimir Propp asserted, 'A writer who mines the treasure of folklore must not only accept the tradition, but overcome it.' Like the Austrian poet Ingeborg Bachmann, who burns through the closing pages of *Music for the Dead*, Mort conjures poetry 'out of the very limits of language'; poetry that circumnavigates Wittgenstein's assertion – 'What we cannot speak about we must consign to silence.' 'Silence bleeds us to language' Mort writes, in 'To Ingeborg Bachmann in Rome'. 'Silence beats language out of us. / Praise your silence, Ingeborg, your hole in the wall.' Praise also to Valzhyna Mort for this powerful book.

Pre-empted Reading

Nelly Sachs, *Flight and Metamorphosis: Poems,* translated by Joshua Weiner with Linda B. Parshall (FSG) $30
Reviewed by Anthony Barnett

Nelly Sachs was awarded the Nobel Prize for Literature in 1966, shared with S. Agnon, which led to the publication by FSG in USA, followed by Jonathan Cape in the UK, of two volumes of translations of most of her poetry, including a verse play: *O The Chimneys* (1967) and *The Seeker* (1970). Five translators were involved, including Michael Hamburger, and Ruth and Matthew Mead. Some of Sachs's discrete books were, somewhat confusingly, spread across the two volumes. There have been a couple of reordered part reissues since, but Joshua Weiner's is the first new substantial translation of a discrete book.

Nelly Sachs's poetry is so dear to me. During a trip to Stockholm in a pre-digital photography age I visited the reconstruction of her tiny apartment, exactly as she had left it, in the basement of The Royal Library. 'May I take photos?' I asked apprehensively. 'Yes', was a surprise, and I began clicking away. An hour later I discovered that I had had no film in the camera. I think that was what I deserved. My request, I felt, had been an intrusion and the gods had said 'No'. But I did manage to get a poem of my own out of the experience.

What to make of Weiner's translations? One might say that many are faultless. Then again one might say that there are some unjustifiable, impermissible even, decisions. For example, there is not one comma in the whole of Sachs's original *Flucht und Verwandlung*. Weiner does not use them often but often enough for them to be noticeable. In fact, Sachs rarely uses commas in any of her work. Clearly, it is important for her that there be no commas: 'traumgebunden die Gebirge / der Toten / übersteigend' becomes in Weiner: 'dreambound, rising over / the mountains / of the dead' but why? If he thinks he is clarifying things I don't think he is. 'Uneinnehmbar / ist eure aus Segen errichtete / Festung / ihr Toten.' becomes in Weiner: 'Impregnable / is your fortress / (you, the dead) / built only of blessings.' Ruth and Matthew Mead in 1970 have: Impregnable / is your fortress / built only of blessing / you dead.' Sachs does make frequent use of end-line dashes. Weiner takes that as a cue to use them where Sachs does not.

Weiner's introduction is highfalutin: 'the mysterious practice of translation [. . .] the rhyme between *home* and *poem*.' Where there has to be an introduction – they are often indulgences, from which translations of poetry may suffer more often than fiction – I look for a minimum of guidance, the barest helpful context, the righting of wrongs. I don't want to have to scribble scathing comments, make strike-through cancellations, rip out offending pages, not buy the book. I don't want my reading pre-empted. I have my own thinking to do. So, if you can bypass Weiner's introduction, etc, and an odd back cover blurb by Durs Grünbein (who thinks Hamburger previously translated these particular poems when all but a handful were the work of the Meads) – 'Thanks to the bilingual edition [. . .] this translation works like a double fingerprint. And it *really* works' – then you might wish to go for this translation.

On a positive note, I would like to take this opportunity to draw attention to a large-format work published in English translation in 2011 by Stanford University Press: Aris Fioretos, *Nelly Sachs, Flight and Metamorphosis: An Illustrated Biography*, which Weiner references. There you will find, among numerous truly wonderful documents, photos of her apartment now reconstructed in The Royal Library, the one my camera missed.

The Fabric They Call Truth

Shara McCallum, *No Ruined Stone* (Peepal Tree Press)
£9.99
Reviewed by Shash Trevett

In *No Ruined Stone,* the product of many years' research both in Edinburgh and Jamaica, Shara McCallum has created a counterfactual narrative in which Robert Burns leaves Scotland for Jamaica in the summer of 1786. He spends ten years on the island, during which time he has a relationship with an enslaved woman called Nancy. Their child, Agnes, is born two years after his arrival and, when seventeen years old, is raped by Charles Douglas, the owner of the plantation. She dies giving birth to a daughter Isabella, the granddaughter of Robert Burns, who in the second part of the book travels to Scotland in the footsteps of her dead grandfather. In *No Ruined Stone* McCallum creates a multi-layered world in which enslaved people and their descendants are given a voice which combats the erasures of time and cultural normative practices. The collection asks questions such as who gets to write their story, whose voice is heard, and can be viewed as a study on the inheritance of words.

Part One focuses on Burns's impressions of life at 'Springbank', the plantation on Jamaica, his letters home to his brother Gilbert, conversations with Charles Douglas, his abolitionist sensibilities and his ultimate impotence to challenge the machinery of slavery. Burns the Romantic poet rejects the inhumanity of slavery while at the same time appropriating the language of suffering of the enslaved: 'misery clings to the hem of my clothes'; 'there is no keener lash' than the torments he feels. In contrast, Part Two focuses on Isabella, a black woman passing for white, married to a white man who is unaware of her true racial identity. Isabella's voice is secretive, a voice which is constantly negotiating not only the enlightened spaces of Edinburgh, but also the closed dark spaces of marriage. The weight of bearing the legacy of slavery – in its most physical manifestation – preoccupies her thoughts, along with the stresses of 'passing' with the ever-present danger of exposure. People she meets are

content
to make my body a map, to chart
any history they desired.

In this moment of the book, Isabella lets them steer her narrative; by the end of her story she is firmly in charge of her own course through time.

The two parts of the collection, although separated by almost thirty years, mirror each other closely, with several poems sharing titles, images and motifs, which helps move the narrative forward. Burns's section begins with a poem titled 'Voyage' in which he writes to Gilbert about the hard passage to Jamaica: disease, sea sickness, 'I was counted dead, / then nearly dead' and on reaching land he was almost 'stark staring mad'. Isabella's section ends with a poem titled 'Voyage' where a sea, calm like a 'sheet of glass' rocks her as she voyages on a return to recover 'the wreckage' of herself; the stars, 'numberless as the souls lost / to the sea's depths' keeping watch. Both sections contain poems titled 'Springbank': Burns's is the last poem he writes before his death, looking back on his time in Jamaica, retelling his first glimpse of the exterior of the house. His is a coloniser's gaze surveying, measuring, accounting for the land with all the riches it promises. Isabella's 'Springbank' provides the reader with details of her life – of her mother's death, of her grandmother Nancy and of how she came to be freed. It recounts the despair of the enslaved within the house: within its walls she was a ghost who reminded her father of the violence he had inflicted on her mother, 'simply evidence. I needed to be erased'.

Linking the two parts is the figure of Nancy. She is the most enigmatic, shadowy figure in the collection: we hear her voice just once, in the poem 'At the Hour of Duppy and Dream, Miss Nancy Speaks'. At all other times we see her through the eyes, hear her through the ears, know her through the words of those whose lives she is companion to. Although her story is not given the space of its own, it is one that is just as developed as Isabella's. We are not told the exact details of the liaison between her and Burns: to what extent was it consensual, to what extent did Burns slip on the mantle of oppressor. We only see her as a young mother guarding her child closely, 'sensing [his] gaze / but will not countenance it'. She 'wields silence / in her body like an axe' and is feared by Charles Douglas who knows 'he cannot rule nor ken her'. After her child's birth she becomes the Obeah woman 'claiming dominion / over life and death', turned to by enslaved women pregnant as a result of rape, holding dominion also over the projected revenue of the plantation. In the second part of the collection she is presented as a grandmother passing for the slave of her granddaughter, but she is already dead by the time Isabella narrates her story. When we finally hear her voice, she speaks from beyond the grave, a duppy laden with the weight of history and memory:

> hear me for I was there
> in the beginning
> witness as you entered
> as you came dusking
> tearing all asunder rending
> the fabric they call Truth.

The orality of the collection – the weaving together of genealogies and geographies – is laid on a masterful foundation of images which pull out (yet don't broadcast) themes of migration, of the middle passage, of race and the sentimental discourse of the abolitionist movement. One of McCallum's gifts is to present Burns, Isabella and Nancy in beautifully realised character portraits clothed in the subtle precision of her rich and evocative poetry. Burns, Isabella and Nancy glimmer and linger with you days after you have finished reading their final words.

What Price An Inner Life?

The Stasi Poetry Circle, Philip Oltermann (Faber) £14.99
Reviewed by Jennifer Thorp

In an environment where the presence of an inner, secret life of any kind was anathema to the probing eyes of the state, poetry would seem to be at best a low priority. But in Soviet-controlled East Germany after the Second World War, Philip Olterman's new book reveals, there was a concerted effort by the Stasi intelligence service to use metre, meaning and metaphor for their own ends. Olterman lays out how unlikely this pairing feels early on:

> What an absurd meeting of mindsets, I had thought at the time: one of the most brutal spy agencies in history on the one hand, the refined craft of lyrical verse on the other. A secret police synonymous with the suppression of free through, and an art form through which men and women had for millennia expressed their innermost feelings and desires. What had attracted one to the other?

The collaboration is more intuitive than it seems. Governments, particularly totalitarian ones, have always had an intense interest in the arts, and in how it can be used or erased to produce a loyal populace with the 'right' kinds of thoughts. Step outside the lines of acceptable art, and the punishments could be brutal: witness Akhmatova's executed husband, Shostakovich's years in exile when the Stalinist state disapproved of *Lady Macbeth of Mtsensk,* or Bulgakov keeping *The Master and Margarita* in a drawer for decades for fear of the gulags. For the East German state, art was a tool like anything else, and the Stasi initially saw their mission clearly: educate young writers in poetic technique, fuel class warfare through their rousing, politically perfect art, everybody wins. Easy.

Except of course it isn't, and Otterman leads us on a strange romp through improbable spaces, from sonnet workshops in the imposing Stasi headquarters to faux-comforting poetry gatherings where young writers' tastes were secretly reported by informants. In a slim volume drawing on archival material, often terrible poems, and interviews with sometimes-reticent ex-poets, he builds an effective picture of a world where friends, lovers and fellow artists informed vociferously on each other, and where every scribbled couplet could lead to brutal danger.

The origins of Stasi poetry circles, Oltermann argues convincingly, lie in the formation of the German Democratic Republic itself. From the ruins left in 1945, idealists declared that they'd form a Germany that once again prioritised *Dichter und Denker,* thinkers and poets. The politician Johannes Becher fervently believed sonnets were a mirror of the Marxist view of historical progress, and that poetry was poised to be at the core of the new state. By the 1970s, the Circle of Writers, with its Stasi-vetted pupils, was fuelled by the hope that high-quality poetic work in a state-monitored environment could help the socialist struggle. But Oltermann traces how these hopes began to warp, as Stasi paranoia and the threat of nuclear war in the 1980s turned the GDR increasingly inward. The Circle itself also fractured, as poets disagreed on the best forms of truly socialist poetry, and started to write work containing inconvenient questions about art and the right to inner struggle.

The volume's focus on personalities is where it really flourishes, from the Circle leader and informant Uwe Berger, who had a nasty habit of complaining to the Stasi when reviews of his work weren't acceptably fawning, to Alexander Ruika, a young poet of promise who was manipulated into informing on other artists at literary gatherings. It also takes the reader on detours into the utterly surreal. The Stasi thought young poets might be hiding improper messages in their work, which isn't a new idea: according to historian Michael Kater, Carl Orff, the composer who collaborated with the Nazis, argued that he was secretly antifascist because he'd hidden anti-Nazi subtexts in *Carmina Burana.* And, improbably, the Stasi weren't off the mark at all. The poet Uwe Kolbe managed to sneak a secret, hilarious acrostic critical of the state right past their censors' noses. This was a world in which imprisoned writer Annegret Rollin could be interrogated thirty-six times over the meaning of one poem, in which the Stasi produced a James Bond equivalent who ran around the world fighting capitalists and bedding blonde Nazis undercover. One poet under Stasi monitoring stepped into a taxi in 1987 and discovered that Ruika was his taxi driver (Ruika claims this was a coincidence). Oltermann's work prepares us for anything, no matter how implausible.

It's an extraordinary feat of research that shows a side of totalitarian thinking rarely seen: its deep-rooted cultural insecurity, in which interpretations outside of the lines are viscerally threatening. The Stasi, Olterman notes, required people in its service to be 'crystal' – absolutely clear to them and opaque to everybody else. Rescuing their poetic efforts from the opacity of history makes for a rewarding, if all-too-brief, read.

A Great Love of Fleas

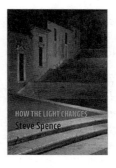

Steve Spence, *How The Light Changes* (Shearsman) £10.95; Steve Spence, *Eat Here, Get Gas & Worms* (Red Ceilings Press) £8.00
Reviewed by Alan Munton

The sentences in these poems do not follow from each other. This does not make things easy for the reader, but it sets up a vital relationship between the text and the hopeful interpreter. Here is an example of what the reader has to confront, from a poem entitled 'Contorting The Clouds' (which nowhere mentions clouds):

> 'It's a virus that's spreading,' he said.
> Truth has become a matter of opinion
> but gravity is still gravity and it's a
>
> symptom of a failing education system.
> Yet the dragonfly is a beautiful beast
> and infinity remains an extraordinary
>
> and puzzling concept. [....] Would you carry
> out surgery on yourself in order to survive?
> (*How The Light Changes*, p.40)

My reason for choosing a poem with that first line will be obvious enough; but it was written in 2017 or before; this is not post-Covid writing, although Covid gives it meaning – to which we can add the striking perception here that for too many people the truth about the pandemic is indeed a matter of opinion. But what does gravity, a failing education system, a dragonfly and infinity have to do with a virus? And what is the effect of the sudden arrival of a potentially cut up body?

An immediate answer is: nothing. These entities simply do not belong together. The poems challenge meaning when continuity is actively denied. This becomes a challenge to our idea of a poem. Spence has been writing in this way since his first book in 2010, *A Curious Shipwreck*, which was shortlisted for the Forward Prize for best first collection. There have been three further books, and the two reviewed here were both published in 2021. This continuity suggests that publishers and readers have not had fundamental problems with his discontinuous verse. For Spence is *quoting*; the language of these poems is not original, it is borrowed. All of it. His texts are generated from what has already been said by someone else. These quotations are extracted from the existing culture, from printed news above all. There is the news heard on radio and television, words and phrases taken from recorded speech, from commentary and opinion of all kinds, even including weather forecasts. The reader hears voices.

And it is the reader of Spence's lines who must create meaning. We can choose a sentence or a phrase and engage with it by putting it into a story that we invent for ourselves. It may give us pleasure, or its opposite. It may give us nothing. The reader is not being asked to engage with the poet's presentation of his or her own subjectivity. The purposive, the intensely personal, are absent; for the poet himself is largely absent. A multitude of questions are asked in these poems: 'Has the world changed?'; 'Are you out and about, seeing what / you can hear?'; 'Have you got the / collecting bug?'. But no answers follow. The reader may want to imagine the context in which such a question could be asked, perhaps invent who might be asking it; or decide what a reply might be, or insert it into their own life. This is divergent writing with a vengeance.

What meaning, then, do these poems have? Quotations removed from their context resemble the chaotic world we live in, where little of what we experience is complete or in a secure relationship with anything else. Spence's poems are a record of our politics and our culture: they often take up phrases with a political content, whether the 'failing education system' from my opening quotation, or the gunshots and famine mentioned in the poem below. And it is always 'them and us'. Altogether, these poems are a record of the language of our time, showing how we experience it and how we might deal with it. Consider, finally, the *Eat Here* poem 'Deciding Where To Stand' with those concepts in mind:

Sometimes there are explosions,
sometimes it's gunshots yet these
innovations are our own and not
everyone has a great love of fleas.

Of course, there is always the
matter of taste but not every
question has an answer and it's
important to understand what

we're being told. 'It all feels so
real,' she said. These people are
chattering in different languages
and it's fun to listen to the sounds

and pick out the occasional word
you might know. Once again famine
is knocking at our door. 'Them and
us' she said, 'it's always them and us.'

This soundtrack has two versions of *99 red balloons*. Yes but are we correcting our previous mistakes?

The Foggy, Foggy Dew

Gallery of Clouds, Rachel Eisendrath (NYRB) £17.99
Reviewed by Andrew Hadfield

A slender, elegant volume inspired by a capacious, rambling prose epic, *Gallery of Clouds* is a work written in response to Sir Philip Sidney's *Arcadia*. Sidney's complicated and episodic work, one that uses its ancient mythical pastoral setting to meditate on the nuanced, overlapping and conflicting relationship between the active and passive life, was extensively revised and exists in three versions. There is the *Old Arcadia*, the most easily readable of the three, discovered in the early twentieth century – although it was known to have existed long before then. After Sidney's early death in 1586 at the age of thirty-one, two rival editions appeared based on his extensive revisions to his original text. His friend, Fulke Greville (1554–1628), oversaw the publication of the *New Arcadia* in 1590, the revised work with its extra sections and plots concluding in mid-sentence. A composite version, which inserts some of the 'Old' into the 'New', as well as adding other sections so that the romance makes sense, was published by Philip's devoted and brilliant sister, Mary Sidney Herbert (1561–1621) three years later. Confusingly, both are called *The Countess of Pembroke's Arcadia*, although the first is an incomplete, pirated edition.

The plot of the later versions involves the withdrawal of king Basilius into a pastoral retreat after he hears a prophecy that he will lose his family and his state to hostile forces. Pyrocles and Musidorus, two impressively noble princes, fall in love with the king's daughters, Pamela and Philoclea, disguising themselves to press their suits. Politics and romance are inextricably intertwined from the start, the complicated interactions of the various love triangles subsequently established often interrupted by attacks from angry mobs of Arcadian citizens dissatisfied by Basilius's neglect of his state. Basilius, in love with Cleophilia (in reality, Pyrocles disguised as a female warrior), dies when he accidently drinks poison meant for Pyrocles, prepared by a rejected female suitor, Gynecia. Pyrocles is imprisoned, as he has played some part in Basilius's death, where he is joined by Musidorus, who had run off with Pamela, leading to them being kidnapped by another angry mob. Chaos reigns in Arcadia, but, fortunately, Eucharus, the ruler of a neighbouring province, comes to visit Basilius, not knowing that his fellow ruler is also his son. He is persuaded to stay and rule Arcadia while Basilius's death is investigated. Gynecia, Pyrocles, and Musidorus all receive the death sentence but, just as they are about to cop it, the 'corpse' of Basilius moves, he is reunited with his father and the princes and princesses can get married and live happily ever after.

The interest of the prose work lies in its style as well as the themes tackled in particular episodes (fate and destiny; reason against passion; identity; political resistance or Stoical endurance), rather than its overall construction, which I have rather sketchily outlined. Rachel Eisendrath, a Renaissance literature professor in New York with an interest in creative writing, has responded to the episodic nature of Sidney's work and adapted ideas from her reading of the *Arcadia*, a work of which she admits, as I do too, she can never remember the story. The *Gallery of Clouds* is not a work of fragments, shards or 'scattered rhymes', but a book of clouds: 'Clouds are ephemeral moments of light and colour and stay still only as long as you look at them, but then – as soon as your mind wanders – change into something else' (pp.4–5). Using this formula as a starting point, or a structural principle, she is then able to range widely throughout her short text, recounting an imagined encounter with Virginia Woolf in heaven where she gives her a manuscript of one of her [Eisendrath's books]; then her first encounter with Sidney's romance in a library; moving on to a recollection of her stepfather reading on a couch in New York; the significance of manicules (little hands drawn in the margins of Renaissance books designed to act as prompts); a visit the Woolfs and Vita Sackville-West made to Penshurst the day the Nazis entered Paris (14 June 1940); reflections on her own career as an academic; one of Spenser's sonnets; reading Willa Cather to her grandmother; the career and significance of Vivian Gordon Harsh (1890–1960), the first African American head librarian in the Chicago public library system; among other subjects.

Professor Eisendrath writes engagingly throughout, and she has a light touch when dealing with the academic subjects that are the staple of her professional life. She recalls C.S. Lewis's advice that the best way to read an Italian romance, the *Arcadia* being a literary 'first cousin on the family's English side... is for eight hours a day in a room by the sea while recovering from a minor illness' (p.9). It is surely good counsel and neatly captures the demands made upon our time by such works of literature, pointing out the need to have patience and leisure to consume them, escaping from the demands and pressures of ordinary life much as Basilius sought to do when retreating into the forests of Arcadia. It also, deliberately, contrasts Eisendrath's gallery of clouds to those of Sir Philip Sidney. His are long reflective discussions of complicated issues designed to weigh up the pros and cons of particular positions within challenging debates; hers, short reflections on subjects that often have little obvious link to the previous or subsequent passage, and which are linked solely through her imagination.

There are some astute reflections on art works and their relationship to romance. The French landscape painter, Jean-Baptiste-Camille Corot (1796–1875), produced a large number of works that contain a red hat. The detail becomes a device, effectively removing the viewer from the scene so that the painting does not become 'a foggy atmosphere, a piece of thick woollen fabric, a scrap of wallpaper, mold on wet twigs, pea soup, some forgotten vegetable in the back of the refrigerator's bottom drawer' (pp.41–2). The *Arcadia*, in contrast, wants the reader to get lost in its enveloping folds and not to escape, which is why it does not contain any red hats and has no words 'telling you to wake up' (p.45). Its rhetoric luxuriates in artificial ornaments. Nicholas Poussin (1594–1665), who painted the most famous representation of Arcadia, *Et in Arcadia Ego* ('even in Arcadia am I' (p.64), as it is translated here), is shown to have brought together two central features of the romance: the discovery of death and the discovery of painting. Accordingly, in Poussin's picture, 'The idyllic landscape of Arcadia is a dream, an escape from death, but, as in a dream, one encounters what is disturbing about reality even there' (p.67).

Professor Eisendrath is invariably an astute companion on the highways and byways of romance. She recounts a lecture she gives to her students at Barnard College in Manhattan. Although she claims that her audience watches her face and does not listen to her words, their soporific reactions in the viscous air of the lecture theatre reflecting the slow sideways movements of romance narratives, on the page the words are insightful and helpful. Romance is about 'vivid retrospection' and whereas epic is about 'doing, acting, overcoming, singing', romance is concerned with 'waiting, enduring, receiving, listening' (p.19). She reflects on books that are forms of romance, such as Walter Benjamin's *Arcades* project, his languid study of the changes to city life and thought generated by the introduction of arcades into Paris in the nineteenth century, and Montaigne's endlessly rewritten *Essays*. Romance, she concludes, is a democratic genre, one in which there is no controlling king or teacher, but in which thoughts link together as if arm in arm, 'weaving through the field' (p.118).

The book is often at its best when the author, whose scholarly monograph was awarded a significant prize, shows off her considerable literary critical talents. The love-stricken Pyrocles is distracted from his melancholy when his host, Kalander, invites him along with Musidorus on a hunt. Hunting was a familiar trope for the pursuit of love and the author explores its significance. Resisting Thomas Wyatt's excessively cited adaptation of Petrarch's sonnet 190, we are directed instead to Edmund Spenser's sonnet, *Amoretti* 67, 'Like as a huntsman after weary chase'. In this poem, one of a sequence in which Spenser recounts his courtship of his second wife, Elizabeth Boyle, the deer escapes the fatigued hunter in the octave, only to return in the sestet and voluntarily surrender to his will. Professor Eisendrath likens the process to difficult literary interpretation, where after an arduous journey involving late nights, early mornings, foreign language classes, discarded drafts, frustration, embarrassment and self-doubt, you give up and admit your failure only to realise that you probably do have some understanding of the work: 'the text comes to you. Gently on her little hooves, she picks her way to you through all the fallen leaves' (p.114). It is perhaps not a surprise that the author states that, for her, 'entering the world of scholarship is like passing through a magic door' (p.104).

I wished that the reflection on Sidney's style had been somewhat longer, as I wanted many of the book's suggestive sections to have more substance. The prose of the *Arcadia* can be read, following the work of the Princeton historian of prose, Morris William Croll, as a work in the 'oratorical style' (p.52), characterised by *schemata verborum*, 'similarities or repetitions of sound used as purely sensuous devices to give pleasure or aid the attention' (p.53). Indeed, it can be regarded as probably the last and most lavish or decadent example of such a style before the advent of more modern, functional prose, characterised by its colloquial, realistic rhythms and phrases. Like the deer hunted in Spenser's sonnet the *Arcadia* is a creature realising its time has come and surrendering, this time not meekly but with the 'distant bellow of a nearly extinct animal' (p.53).

Gallery of Clouds is often an enjoyable book. It finishes on a rather whimsical note, I thought: 'Why do animals not look at clouds? Could this be a feature that characterizes the human – that we have a psychic need for clouds? At certain hours, even people on the streets of New York look up' (p.135). One suspects not, and, even if it were a plausible case, the reader might need something of greater substance here. Even though the 1590 Greville *et al Arcadia* ends in mid-sentence – 'Whereat ashamed, (as having never done so much before in his life)' – it is hard to read anything into this lacuna other than bad production editing, just as it is something of a stretch to see Sir Philip deliberately striking a similar note in his prose or poetry.

There seems to be something of a fashion for hybrid books, works that deal with a subject but which also emphasise the nature of the author's own thinking, quest for knowledge, or fine writing. For some reason they often appeal to academics, eager it seems to connect to a wider culture of memoir and personal reflection. I have my doubts about the value of such labour: the purpose is surely to go beyond a limited university context and to connect with a wider public, generating not merely sales – there is probably not vast wealth to be gained here – but also showing the value of the humanities to more people and, with any luck, persuading them to follow their own journeys into past literature, history and culture. Some work, but, one suspects, very few, and more often than not, something is produced that is neither flesh nor fowl, that mixes author and subject in a manner that produces very little knowledge about either. It is hard to see many surviving long beyond their original print run or readers returning to them a few years later for help and insight.

As this review demonstrates, *Gallery of Clouds* has far more substance than most and it demonstrates that its author is a perceptive critic, engaging writer and a fine teacher. I do wonder whether a critical work on Sidney might have performed more useful labours, a work of fiction, or, something more auto/biographical.

Points of Departure

Helen Bowell, *The Barman* (Bad Betty Press) £7
Eve Esfandiari-Denney, *My Bodies This Morning This Evening* (Bad Betty Press) £7
Jess McKinney, *Weeding* (Hazel Press) £10
Manuela Moser, *Last night, the mountain* (Bad Betty Press) £7
Reviewed by Joe Carrick-Varty

I love a pamphlet. Especially a debut pamphlet. That fast-coming adage of 'EP before album' just works. Here we are at the beginning or, not really the *beginning* beginning, there's so much that happens before a pamphlet comes out – maybe a degree, magazine publication, tweeting etc. – but the beginning in terms of any kind of homogeneous collection of work). These are a poet's first breaths, first steps into the mode of book publication, of fashioning ideas into a discernible complete thought, and pushing pages into the world. It's newness... and newness, for any reader, is revitalising.

Helen Bowell's pamphlet *The Barman* (Bad Betty Press, 2022) is, amongst many things, a cross section of a relationship. At one moment funny and heart-breaking: 'Can I give you this trout for safe-keeping?', the next frank and arresting: 'I had a dream the barman couldn't find his favourite pen / and called me a slanty-eyed thief', the poems offer up truths, illuminating the many angles of a problematic romantic relationship, for all the toxicity and joy and nostalgia and hopelessness, and I loved them for it.

Brilliant images like 'the nine drunk selfies / we snapped early on... after last orders, our teeth still / white and hard as promises' orbit a shadow, a darkness, that rears its head with shocking clarity, as in 'Scaredy Barman': 'One time a man spray-painted WHORE / on my friend's house while she slept.' And it's the moments when these darknesses are set into relief that really got me, when they collide with light, as in 'Summer': 'We laze before the telly and through the windows / the great flash photographer in the sky does their work.'

When describing Manuela Moser's work, Padraig Regan says: 'This poetry may not be easy to understand, but it is easy to love', and I agree. Moser's pamphlet, enigmatically titled *Last night, the mountain* (Bad Betty Press, 2021), finds its home in the act of experience and re-experience. Moser uses memory, but not in an anecdotal way, more as a means to measure hairline fractures between this and that, as in 'Not an exact measurement', when a deer is shot and frozen in time: 'Only by seeing it, dead... did we understand... Unmistakably a deer, glimpsed through trees, upright and then not.' And there is something growing deep down between these interstices.

Moser's poetry feels entirely its own; the voice, constantly asserting and reasserting itself, excited me: 'One of your responsibilities is to think of yourself as alone... Most of what you understand is wrong'. Enigmatic and difficult as this pamphlet might be, it's also full of cracking one-liners, such as: 'Last night the mountain looked like crushed velvet against the sky'.

Eve Esfandiari-Denney's pamphlet *My Bodies This Morning This Evening* (Bad Betty Press, 2022) is an exploration of what it means to be a person, to have a body (with all its limitations), and, despite everything, to love. This pamphlet gleams in its ability to balance vulnerability with awe, as in the final poem 'vultures are singing': 'I am seventeen and dying of cancer' and the first poem 'Sunbird doubting': 'I want to be daylight without a witness'.

I love poetry that admits it isn't in control, poetry that doesn't profess to be omniscient. The speakers of *My Bodies* are anything but omniscient, but they relish their unknowing as they track themes of mixed heritage and life-threatening illness, all from the most intimate of distances: 'Did I miss the turning into the sun... When I tried on love like a wetsuit'.

It's hard to be moving and funny in one poem, but Esfandiari-Denney manages this time and time again, none more so than in '~This Is Medium World 7~', which begins: 'Myself and then my body are / sipping sequin-coloured Oxy through / a vein on the edge of light', before giving us '*that absolute / classic Ibiza tune*', and then 'the horses from the Lloyds TSB advert', and ending with:

i was so sad when they folded me back
into the sheets of the portable bed returning
to a room dying could enter

Jess McKinney's pamphlet *Weeding* (Hazel Press, 2021) is punctuated with colour, specifically the colour green, which, it turns out, is also the colour of love: 'The colour of my foot touching your own tender arch unflinching in bed.'

Constantly surprising with its turn of voice (from birds 'melt[ing] into a singular animal, swoop[ing] like the beating heart of pointillism', to 'I've had some of my best epiphanies in a room with a sink' [yes!]), this pamphlet revels in its keen ability to look one step further, as in 'Olive', when McKinney offers the image of artichoke hearts, specifically the green of artichoke hearts, but shows more, flies higher, and in such a short distance: 'I want to know the green that was beating with the life of a thousand little artichoke hearts'. And of course, now I also want to know this beating, to feel its colour against my skin, to 'bliss out to the hum of insects buzzing in the distance.'

Some Contributors

Louis Klee is an Australian writer. He is currently a fellow at Clare College, Cambridge. **Anthony Barnett**'s work is celebrated on the occasion of his eightieth birthday by Caroline Clark and many others in *PNR* 262. **Martin Caseley** writes essays, book reviews and short prose pieces for several journals, including *PN Review* and *Agenda*. He lives in Norfolk and also contributes to the website International Times and Review 31. **Jeremy Page**'s latest publications are *London Calling* and *Other Stories* (Cultured Llama, 2018) and *The Naming* (Frogmore Press, 2021). He edits *The Frogmore Papers* from Lewes, East Sussex. **Dean Browne** won the Geoffrey Dearmer Prize in 2021 and his pamphlet, *Kitchens at Night*, was a winner of the Poetry Business International Pamphlet Competition; it was published by Smith|-Doorstop in 2022. His poems have appeared in *Banshee*, *Poetry* (Chicago), *Poetry Ireland Review*, *Poetry Review*, *Southword*, *Stinging Fly*. **Andrew Hadfield** is a Professor of English at the University of Sussex and a Fellow of the British Academy. *Thomas Nashe and Late Elizabethan Writing* will be published by Reaktion later this year. **Jennifer Thorp** is a librettist and novelist who received a PhD on art and totalitarian regimes from the University of Manchester in 2014. Her first novel, *Learwife*, was published by Canongate in 2021. **Shash Trevett** is a British-Tamil originally from Sri Lanka. Her pamphlet *From a Borrowed Land* was published by Smith|Doorstop (2021) and she is a Ledbury Critic. **Joe Carrick-Varty** is a British-Irish writer, editor and co-founder of *bath magg*. His debut collection is forthcoming in 2023. **Betsy Rosenberg** was born in Philadelphia and lives in Jerusalem where she works as a translator and editor. A book of her selected poems, *A Future More Vivid*, was published by Sheep Meadow Press. **Toon Tellegen** (1941) is one of Holland's most celebrated poets. He has written more than twenty collections to date. His collection *Raptors* (Carcanet) won the Popescu Prize in 2011. **Judith Wilkinson** is a poet and award-winning translator. She is currently translating Tellegen's latest collection. Her own collection *In Desert* was recently published by Shoestring. **Nicki Heinen**'s debut collection *There May Not Be a Reason Why* is out now with Verve Press. She identifies as disabled, living with bipolar disorder. She lives in London. **James Geary**, deputy curator of the Nieman Foundation for Journalism at Harvard, was Alvin Feinman's student in the 1980s. His most recent book is *Wit's End: What Wit Is, How It Works, and Why We Need It*. **William Wootten**'s 2021 pamphlet *Looking at the Horsemen* is published by New Walk. His 2016 collection *You Have a Visitor* is published by Worple.

Editors
Michael Schmidt
John McAuliffe

Editorial Manager
Andrew Latimer

Contributing Editors
Vahni Capildeo
Sasha Dugdale
Will Harris

Proofreader
Maren Meinhardt

Designer
Andrew Latimer

Editorial address
The Editors at the address on the right. Manuscripts cannot be returned unless accompanied by a stamped addressed envelope or international reply coupon.

Trade distributors
NBN International

Represented by
Compass ips Ltd

Copyright
© 2022 Poetry Nation Review
All rights reserved
ISBN 978-1-80017-283-8
ISBN 0144-7076

Subscriptions—6 issues
  INDIVIDUAL–print and digital:
£45; abroad £65
  INSTITUTIONS–print only:
£76; abroad £90
  INSTITUTIONS–digital only:
from Exact Editions (https://shop. exacteditions.com/gb/pn-review) to: PN Review, Alliance House, 30 Cross Street, Manchester, M2 7AQ, UK.

Supported by

Supported using public funding by
ARTS COUNCIL ENGLAND